my revision notes

AQA GCSE

ENGLISH LANGUAGE

Keith Brindle

HODDER
EDUCATION
AN HACHETTE UK COMPANY

The publisher would like to thank the following for permission to reproduce copyright material:

Acknowledgements: **p.10: Ian Rankin:** From *Knots and Crosses* (Orion, 1999); **pp.12, 74: Brady Udall:** From *The Miracle Life of Edgar Mint* (Jonathan Cape, 2001); **pp.13, 91: M. L. Steadman:** From *The Light Between Oceans* by M. L. Steadman, published by Doubleday. Reproduced by permission of The Random House Group Ltd.; **p.14: Harper Lee:** From *To Kill a Mockingbird* (Arrow Books, 2006); **p.16: Roald Dahl:** From 'Claud's Dog' (Penguin, 1953) © Roald Dahl. Reproduced by permission of the publisher; **p.16: Daphne du Marier:** From 'The Birds', in *The Birds and Other Stories* (Penguin, 1975); **p.18: Dean R. Koontz:** From *The Face of Fear* (Headline, 1989); **p.18: Tom Sharpe:** From *Wilt on High* (Secker and Warburg, 1984); **p.19: David Lodge:** From *The British Museum is Falling Down* by David Lodge, published by Secker (Random House, 1965), reproduced by permission of The Random House Group Ltd.; **pp.20, 90: Nick Hornby:** From *High Fidelity* (Penguin, 1995), reproduced by permission of the publisher; **p.21: Ray Bradbury:** From *The Day it Rained Forever* (Penguin, 1969); **p.21: Ernest Hemmingway:** From *A Farewell to Arms* (Scribner, 1929); **p.21: Isla Dewar:** From *Women Talking Dirty* (Headline, 2002); **p.22: Ben Elton:** From *Blind Faith* by Ben Elton, published by Bantam Press. Reproduced by permission of The Random House Group Ltd.; **p.23: Robert Swindells:** From *Stone Cold* (Heinemann, 1997); **p.24: Dan Brown:** From *Angels and Demons* (Pocket Star Books, 2001); **p.25: Isla Dewar:** From *Two Kinds of Wonderful* (Headline: 2001), reproduced by permission of the publisher; **pp.26, 27, 91: Farrukh Dhondy:** From *Come to Mecca* (Cascades, 1983); **pp. 28,29: Naomi Mitchison:** From 'The Hostages', in *A Book of Modern Stories* (Oxford University Press, 1974); **pp.30, 82: F. Scott Fitzgerald:** From *The Great Gatsby* (Penguin, 1971), reproduced by permission of the publisher; **p.32: H. Drake Brockman:** From 'Fear' in *A Book of Modern Stories* (Oxford University Press, 1974); **p.34: Nick Hornby:** From *About a Boy* (Indigo, 1999), reproduced by permission of the publisher; **p.37: William Sitwell:** From 'A lazy, vulgar rip-off – it's time to ban brunch', *The Daily Telegraph* (22 October 2014) © Telegraph Media Group Limited 2014; **p.38: Jane Purves:** From 'The Queen's Dinner', *The Woman's Magazine Annual* (1935); **p.39: Hermione Hoby:** From 'I learned how to be a person writing this thing', *The New Review* (17 August 2014) Copyright Guardian News & Media Ltd 2015; **p.40: Alexis de Tocqueville:** From 'Democracy in America', *The Receiving End* (Penguin, 1973), reproduced by permission of the publisher; **pp.42, 48: Mike Harding:** From *Hypnotising the Cat* (Robson Books, 1995); **p.44:** From *Irish Catholic Chronicle And People's News of the Week* (2 November 1876); **p.44: Peter Hitchins:** From *Mail Online* (22 December 2014); **p.46: Chief Joseph:** from www.artofmanliness.com/2008/08/01/the-35-greatest-speeches-in-history (1877); **p.47: Lauren Laverne:** From *The Observer Magazine* (30 November 2014) Copyright Guardian News & Media Ltd 2015; **p.47: Hannah Furness:** From 'Witchmarks, gunpowder plot and paranoia – secrets under the floorboards', *The Daily Telegraph* (5 November 2014) © Telegraph Media Group Limited 2014; **p.48: Michael McIntyre:** From *Life and Laughing* (Penguin, 2010), reproduced by permission of the publisher; **p.49–50: Bill Cosby:** From *Fatherhood* (Bantam Press, 1987); **p.50–1:** From https://archive.org/stream/nineteenthcentu00reesgoog#page/n55/mode/2u (1835); **p.51: Camara Laye:** From *Dark Child* (Penguin, 1970); **p.52: Nathan Blake:** From *Wales Online* www.walesonline.co.uk/sport/sport-opinion/nathan-blake-fighting-way-through-8159232 (24 November 2014); **p.53: Charles Sumner:** From *Barbarism of Slavery* https://archive.org/stream/barbarismofslave00lcsumn#page/8/mode/2up (1863); **p.54: George Anderson:** From http://digital.nls.uk/emigration/communities/george-anderson/letter-1891.html (1891); **p.54–5:** www.footprinttravelguides.com/latin-america/argentina/patagonia/southern-atlantic-coast/puerto-san-julian; **p.57:** From *Daily News* (November 1888); **p.58: George Sims:** From *The Mysteries of Modern London, 1906* (Random House); **p.58: Cynthia Dusel-Bacon:** From *Bear Attacks, their causes and avoidance* (Hurtig Publishers, 1985); **p.58–9:** From *The Indiana Weekly Progress* (1886); **p.72: Leslie Charteris:** From *Follow the Saint* (Hodder, 1938), reproduced by permission of the publisher; **p.76: John Steinbeck:** From *Of Mice and Men* (Penguin, 1971); **p.77: Keith Waterhouse:** From *There is a Happy Land* (Longman, 1968) © Keith Waterhouse. Reproduced by permission of the publisher; **p.78: Ed Helmore:** From 'From spreading happiness to saving the planet, the rise and rise of Pharell', *The Observer* (25 January 2015) Copyright Guardian News & Media Ltd 2015; **p.80: David Storey:** From *Saville* (Vintage, 1998); **p.87: J. D. Salinger:** From *The Catcher in the Rye* (Little Brown, 1951); **p.88: Salman Rushdie:** From *East, West* (BCA, 1994); **p.91: Stan Barstow:** From *The Human Element* (The Human Element, 1972); **p.92: Clifford Simak:** From *Way Station* (Pan, 1963); **p.93: Ben Elton:** From *Dead Famous* (Black Swan, 2001); **p.93: James Herbert:** From *Moon* (Pan, 1985); **pp. 97–8: Andrew Anthony:** From 'The naked rambler is making us look silly', *The Observer* www.theguardian.com/commentisfree/2010/jan/17/naked-rambler-terror-arrest (17 January 2010) Copyright Guardian News & Media Ltd 2015; **p.101: Phil Hogan:** From www.theguardian.com/tv-and-radio/2014/aug/23/doctor-who-horizon-the-honourable-woman-tv-review (23 August 2014) Copyright Guardian News & Media Ltd 2015; **pp.101–2: Bob Morgan:** From *The Huffington Post* www.huffingtonpost.co.uk/bob-morgan/uk-police-armed_b_1895947.html (19 September 2012)

Photo credits: p.81 © xy – Fotolia; **p.85** © Antonio Gravante – Fotolia; **p.87** © ViewApart – Fotolia; **p.94** © Aania – Fotolia

Although every effort has been made to ensure that website addresses are correct at time of going to press, Hodder Education cannot be held responsible for the content of any website mentioned. It is sometimes possible to find a relocated web page by typing in the address of the home page for a website in the URL window of your browser.

Orders: please contact Bookpoint Ltd, 130 Milton Park, Abingdon, Oxon OX14 4SB. Telephone: (44) 01235 827720. Fax: (44) 01235 400454. Lines are open 9.00–17.00, Monday to Saturday, with a 24-hour message answering service. Visit our website at www.hoddereducation.co.uk

© Keith Brindle 2015

First published in 2015 by

Hodder Education

An Hachette UK Company,

Carmelite House, 50 Victoria Embankment

London EC4Y 0DZ

Impression number	5	4	3	
Year	2019	2018	2017	2016

Cover photo © Shockfactor – fotolia.com

Illustrations by Integra Software Services Pvt. Ltd., Pondicherry, India

Typeset in Bembo Std Regular 11/13 by Integra Software Services Pvt. Ltd., Pondicherry, India

Printed in Spain by Graphycems

A catalogue record for this title is available from the British Library

ISBN 9781471832055

Get the most from this book

Everyone has to decide his or her own revision strategy, but it is essential to practise the vital skills and develop your understanding. These Revision Notes will help you to do that in a planned way, question by question. Use this book as the cornerstone of your revision and don't hesitate to write in it — personalise your notes and check your progress by ticking off each section as you revise.

Tick to track your progress

Use the revision planner on pages 4 and 5 to plan your revision, topic by topic. Tick each box when you have:
- revised and understood a topic
- tested yourself
- practised exam questions and gone online to check the Test Yourself answers.

You can also keep track of your revision by ticking off each topic heading in the book. You may find it helpful to add your own notes as you work through each topic; highlight points on which you know you need to focus and check your progress.

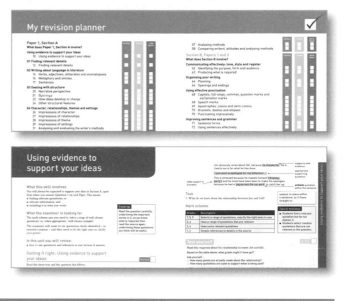

Features to help you succeed

Exam tips

Expert tips are given throughout the book to help you polish your exam technique in order to maximise your chances in the exam.

Typical mistakes

You learn about the typical mistakes candidates make, so you can avoid them.

Test yourself

These activities test how well you have absorbed the advice in the unit. The answers are online.

Definitions of key terms

Clear, concise definitions of essential key terms are provided where they first appear.

Graded answers

Graded example student answers that show you what is required and can make sure you improve still further.

Assessment comment

Throughout, there are comments and annotations which explain exactly why grades are awarded and what is good about the responses that are provided.

How to prepare for the exam

Exam advice is provided for each topic. Use it to consolidate your revision and practise your exam skills.

Online

Go online to check your answers to the Test Yourself activities at **www.hoddereducation.co.uk/ myrevisionnotes/gcse-english-language**

My revision planner

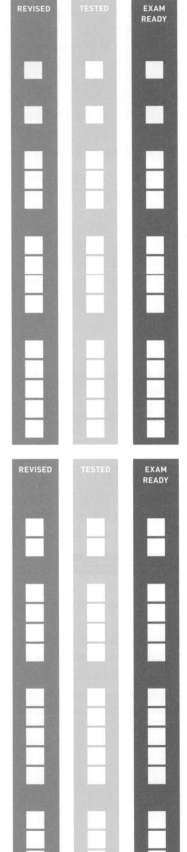

REVISED   TESTED   EXAM READY

REVISED TESTED EXAM READY

REVISED TESTED EXAM READY

Introduction

Welcome to *My Revision Notes for AQA GCSE English Language*.

This book is designed to reinforce the skills required for success in the examination, moving through the different questions and pointing out how to impress the examiner. There are also skills units, focusing on those special areas that are rewarded in the mark schemes.

Here we follow the same pattern as you find in the Student Books for classroom use. There is essential information; and there are annotated and graded answers and further practice tasks so that you can consolidate your learning and develop your potential. In each unit, you can judge what you have produced against the demands of the mark schemes; and, crucially, there are:
- Exam Tips
- lists of Typical Mistakes to avoid
- Key Terms you will need
- test Yourself sections, so you can see the progress you are making.

You can also go online to check how well you are doing at www.hoddereducation.co.uk/myrevisionnotes/gcse-english-language

The book links closely to the *AQA GCSE English Language Workbook*, which will further support what you are learning here. In the Workbook, there is the same pattern of units but more intensive practice: on the web, you will find answers and mark schemes for all the activities.

Both books aim to be fun to work with. The texts and tasks have been selected to offer range and interest, so that you can enjoy the preparation as well as develop your skills and improve your grades.

Also, both books offer short, precise practices in clear, targeted units and are based on the same idea: if you know what the examiner is looking for and you prepare properly for your Big Day, you are much more likely to do well.

If you work through the information and tasks and respond to the advice offered, you can enter the exam room feeling confident, knowing exactly how to respond to each task and how to demonstrate your ability so that the examiner can reward you highly.

We are aiming for improvement and success!

Good luck with your revision!

Keith Brindle

Keith Brindle

What you have to do in the exam ✓

The exam papers

You will have to complete two examination papers.
Each lasts for 1 hour and 45 minutes.

Paper 1

Section A:
- there will be 4 questions based on an extract from a modern novel.
- you will have 1 hour to answer them.

Section B:
- you will be offered 2 essay questions, but must only answer 1 of them.
- you will have to write to describe or to narrate (tell a story).
- you will have 45 minutes to complete the section.

Paper 2

Section A:
- again there will be 4 questions, but in this case they will be based on two non-fiction texts.
- one of the texts will be from the nineteenth century.
- you will have 1 hour to answer the questions.

Section B:
- there will be just 1 question, asking you to give your point of view on a given topic.
- you will have 45 minutes to complete the writing.

All the following skills will be tested

Across the Section As, you will be tested on your ability to:
- find information and link evidence from different texts
- comment on how writers use language and structure for effect
- use subject terminology to support your views
- compare writers' ideas and how they present them
- judge texts critically and support what you say with evidence from the texts.

In the Section Bs, you will be tested on your ability to:
- communicate clearly and effectively
- write appropriately for purpose and audience
- organise your writing effectively
- use a range of vocabulary and sentence structures
- spell and punctuate accurately.

Countdown to my exams

6–8 weeks to go

- Focus on the information on page 7, so you know exactly what the exam involves.
- Read through the revision planner on pages 4 and 5 to familiarise yourself with the skills you need to develop.
- Begin to work through the sections in this book – perhaps using 40 minute sessions once or twice a week. Tick off the sections as you complete them.
- Pay particular attention to the 'How to prepare for the exam' advice and add those practices to your revision.
- In particular, note the revision strategies on pages 104 and 105 and try to spend a minimum of five minutes every day on specific skills development.

REVISED ☐

2–6 weeks to go

- Continue to work through this book and keep doing the five-minute practices too.
- Test your understanding of each topic by working through the 'Test Yourself' questions in the book. Check your answers online.
- Identify the areas in which you have weaknesses. Go back through those sections in this book and prioritise those areas for extra revision work.
- Ask your teacher for help with anything you find especially tricky.
- Track your progress using the revision planner and give yourself a reward when you have achieved your target.
- Attend any revision classes put on by your teacher. Remember, he or she is an expert at preparing people for examinations.

REVISED ☐

One week to go

- Use this book to check again any areas in which you still have weaknesses.
- Continue your five-minute practices.
- Use your teacher to provide any extra input, clarification or advice you need.

REVISED ☐

The day before the examination

- Flick through these Revision Notes for useful reminders, for example, the Exam Tips, exam summaries, Typical Mistakes and Key Terms.
- Check the time and place of your examination.
- Make sure you have everything you need — extra pens and pencils, tissues, a watch, bottled water, sweets.
- Allow some time to relax and have an early night to ensure you are fresh and alert for the examinations.

REVISED ☐

My exams

GCSE English Language Paper 1

Date:..

Time:..

Location:..

GCSE English Language Paper 2

Date:..

Time:..

Location:..

What does Paper 1, Section A involve?

What you have to do ...

The AQA examination papers are very predictable, so it is relatively easy for you to prepare and then to perform well on the day. You just need to know what you are doing!

Paper 1, Section A has four questions about an extract from a novel written in the twentieth or twenty-first century. There are 40 marks available.

You have about an hour to complete this section. It's important that you finish in 60 minutes, because you need the remaining 45 minutes to write your response to Section B.

You must be prepared to spend up to 15 minutes reading the text carefully, then about 45 minutes answering the 4 questions on it. Obviously, the quicker you can read, the more time you will have to answer.

Hopefully, in 15 minutes you will have time to:
- read the text carefully
- read the questions
- read the text through again, with the questions in mind
before you start on Question 1.

The questions will be as follows:

Q1	4 marks	You will have to find 4 details in the first part of the text and list them.
Q2	8 marks	This is the language question. You will be asked how the writer uses language for a particular purpose – perhaps to set the scene – in a section of the text.
Q3	8 marks	This question is on the structure of the text: how the writer has organised the writing.
Q4	20 marks	This question will ask you how the writer has created a particular impression – of the characters, or the setting or whatever – and how you feel about what you have read.

As a rough guide, spend as many minutes writing as there are marks for the question – plus 1! So, for example, 8 marks means 8 or 9 minutes to answer – though if you are a quick reader, you might have a few minutes extra 'in hand' to use when you are answering. In that case, you might be able to spare 10 minutes.

Question 1 is slightly different, but in each of the other questions you will be expected to make points, support them with evidence from the text and explain your ideas.

There are no marks for spelling, sentences or punctuation on this section, but the more clearly you can express yourself, the easier it is for the examiner to understand your ideas and reward your efforts.

Using evidence to support your ideas

What this skill involves

You will always be expected to support your ideas in Section A, apart from when you answer Question 1 on each Paper. This means:
- finding relevant quotations; or
- relevant information; and
- including it in what you write.

What the examiner is looking for

The mark scheme says you need to 'select a range of well-chosen quotations' or, when appropriate, 'well-chosen examples'.

The examiner will want to see quotations clearly identified – in inverted commas – and they need to be the right ones to clarify your points.

Exam tip

Read the question carefully, underlining the important words in it, so you know what is required; then read the source again, underlining those quotations you think will be useful.

In this unit you will revise:
- how to use quotations and references in your Section A answers.

Getting it right: Using evidence to support your ideas

REVISED

Read this short text and the question that follows.

'Gill!'

He caught her as she was getting into her car.

'Hello, Jim.' Cold, businesslike.

'Listen, I just want to apologise for my behaviour at the party.' He was out of breath after a brief jog across the car park, and the words came slowly from his burning chest. 'I mean, I was a bit drunk. Anyway, sorry.'

But Gill knew him too well, knew that this was merely a prelude to a question or request. Suddenly, she felt a little sorry for him, sorry for his fair thick hair which needed a wash, sorry for his short, stocky – she had once thought it powerful – body, for the way he trembled now and again as though cold. But the pity soon wore off. It had been a hard day.

Ian Rankin, *Knots and Crosses*, 1987

Task

1 What does this tell us about Jim?

On the next page is an extract from a Grade 7 answer:

Crucially, quotations are used to show the student has clear understanding.

Jim obviously cares about Gill, because he chases her. He is clearly sorry for what he has done:

'I just want to apologise for my behaviour ...'

This is stressed because he repeats himself ('Anyway, sorry.') and he must have been keen to make his apologies because he had a 'jog across the car park' to catch her up.

supports with evidence

appropriate supporting quotation

adds support in brackets

embeds quotation within the sentence

Task

1 What do we learn about the relationship between Jim and Gill?

Mark scheme

Grades	Descriptors
7, 8, 9	Selects a range of quotations, exactly the right ones to use
5, 6	Uses a range of quotations that are relevant
3, 4	Uses some relevant quotations
1, 2	Simple references to details in the source

> **embed**: to place within a sentence, so it flows straight on

Typical mistakes

- Students find a relevant quotation but do not explain it.
- Students select random quotations that are not relevant to the question.

Test yourself

TESTED

Read this response about the relationship between Jim and Gill.

Based on the table above, what grade might it have got?

Ask yourself:
- How many points are actually made about the relationship?
- How many quotations are used to support what is being said?

We suspect that the relationship has run its course. It's clear that Jim is still chasing her (quite literally!): 'He was out of breath after a brief jog across the car park'. However, he must have behaved badly, since he apologises for his 'behaviour at the party' and knows he was 'a bit drunk'. Because he is asking for forgiveness, she seems to be the one in control.

Gill seems to have had enough of him. At first, she is 'Cold, businesslike', as if she does not want any personal feelings to come between them; but they must have been close, because 'she knew him well' and knows what is likely to come next ('a question or a request'). Actually, she is sympathetic enough to feel sorry for him. She notices his dirty hair, his short body, and 'the way he trembled now and again as though cold'. Presumably, he is not cold, so this suggests he is nervous around her, but she remains detached and does not allow herself to soften towards him: 'the pity soon wore off'.

How to prepare for the exam

You need to practise identifying the right quotations to support your ideas.

So you could:
- read the report of a sports event, decide which team seems to have been the best, then underline the quotations you could use to prove it
- read a review of last night's television programmes, decide which one the reviewer liked most (or least), and underline the quotations you could use as evidence
- read a magazine article about a star, then underline the quotations that tell the reader whether the star is someone we should idolise, or not.

Exam tip

Avoid just saying what happens in a source. Make sure you are answering the question and using evidence wisely, not just copying out sections of text to no purpose.

Paper 1, Q1 Finding relevant details

What this question involves

You will have to list four details that you have found in the opening section of the fiction source. You might, for example, be told to find four things about a character, or the setting, or the weather.

You can:
- quote directly, or
- put the ideas into your own words.

There is no trick in this question: you are likely to be finding **explicit** information that is clearly stated. However, you will also get marks if you find things that are being suggested.

> **explicit**: clearly stated – leaving no room for doubt

Timing

You will have read the source already.

There are 4 marks for this question: ideally, you need to complete it in 4 or 5 minutes.

What the examiner is looking for

There needs to be a simple list of details or quotations.

The only requirements are that what you list:
- is relevant to the question

or, if you are putting an idea into your own words,
- can be verified from the source.

> **Exam tip**
>
> Read the question carefully, then the specified section of the source. Underline the details you think will answer the question. If you have underlined more than four, you can then decide which are the best ones to use.

In this unit you will revise:
- how to locate the necessary information.

Getting it right: Finding relevant details

REVISED ☐

Read this text about a girl (Sunny).

> She laughed again, and as she did she leaned into me and I felt her slick face touching mine and I turned just enough that our mouths were lined up and she kissed me, a soft wet movement of flesh that sent a tingling all the way to my toes. Her fingertips moved like raindrops over the peaks and valleys and plains of my head. The wind lifted her hair up on each side of our faces, leaving us, for a moment, in a small contained space, the only sound the moist friction of our lips.
>
> She pulled away and scooted a few inches away from me on the steps. I felt as if I had no strength in me at all and I wanted to let myself fall into her, like an exhausted man falling into a feather bed, but somehow I managed to keep myself upright. For a while, neither of us said anything. We looked out into the blue darkness and listened to the wind.
>
> Sunny made a funny, hiccupping laugh and stood up. Before she went inside she said, 'Well, at least I kissed somebody tonight.'
>
> *The Miracle Life of Edgar Mint*, Brady Udall, 2001

> **Typical mistakes**
>
> You will not be rewarded if you:
> - select details from the wrong part of the source
> - include points that are not relevant.

Task

1 Which are the four correct things about Sunny that you could have used as your answers?

A She kissed him

B Their mouths 'were lined up'

C Her fingertips moved like raindrops over his head

D She has long hair

E He had no strength in him at all

F Sunny had hiccups

G She lets him pull away from her

H She said, 'Well, at least I kissed somebody tonight'

Mark scheme

You do not need to worry about explaining anything.

You will be given one mark, up to a total of four, for each:

● correct point you make

and/or

● relevant quotation you write down.

In this case, hopefully, you selected A, C, D, H.

In the case of D, 'She has long hair' is not actually stated in the passage. However, it says, 'The wind lifted her hair up on each side of our faces', so the hair cannot have been short.

In this instance, you are finding **implicit** meaning. You will still get the mark, because the point can be verified from the passage.

Next, read the extract below.

> The following night, when the nightmares were worse than usual, Tom decided to escape them by walking the decks. It was two a.m. He was free to wander wherever he wanted at that hour, so he paced methodically, watching the moonlight leave its wake on the water. He climbed to the upper deck, gripping the stair rail to counter the gentle rolling, and stood a moment at the top, taking in the freshness of the breeze and the steadiness of the stars that showered the night.
>
> Out of the corner of his eye, he saw a glimmer come on in one of the cabins. Even first-class passengers had trouble sleeping sometimes, he mused.

M L Stedman, *The Light Between Oceans*, 2012

Task

Question: **Find four things we know about what it was like on the boat that night**.

1 Decide why each of the following points would **not** be correct:

○ Tom was having nightmares.

○ It was two a.m.

○ He paced methodically.

○ He stood at the top of the stairs to the upper deck.

> **Exam tip**
>
> Keep glancing back at the question, to make sure that what you are listing is exactly what the question demands.

> **implicit**: something suggested but not clearly stated

Test yourself

TESTED ☐

Find four details in the extract which are correct and tell us what it was like on the boat.

How to prepare for the exam

Read the openings of novels or short stories.

Each time, ask yourself: what do I learn here about the person or the setting that is being described?

Find four things you could list as your answer.

Paper 1, Q2 Writing about language in literature

What this question involves

You will be asked about how language has been used in a section of the fiction source. You might be asked about how the scene or a character is presented.

Ideally, you will write about:
- words and phrases
- language features and techniques
- sentence forms.

Timing

You will already have read the source.

There are 8 marks for this question, which you will need to complete in 8 or 9 minutes.

What the examiner is looking for

The examiner is hoping you will have:
- **analysed** the language used
- supported what you say with quotations
- used **subject terminology** well.

In this unit you will revise:

how to write about:
- verbs, adjectives, alliteration and onomatopoeia
- metaphors and similes
- sentences.

> **analysis**: explaining in detail – possibly offering more than one interpretation
>
> **subject terminology**: the specialised words to describe language use – e.g. simile, metaphor and complex sentence

Getting it right: Verbs, adjectives, alliteration and onomatopoeia

REVISED ☐

This is a description of a town in southern America.

> Maycombe was an old town, but it was a tired old town when I first knew it. In rainy weather, the streets turned to red slop; grass grew on the sidewalks, the courthouse sagged in the square. Somehow, it was hotter then: a black dog suffered on a summer's day; bony mules flicked flies in the sweltering shade on the square. Men's stiff collars wilted by nine in the morning ...
>
> Harper Lee, *To Kill a Mockingbird*, 1960

Task

1 Complete these lists of:
   - all the **adjectives** used: 'old', 'tired', 'rainy' ...
   - the powerful **verbs** used: 'sagged', 'suffered' ...

> **adjective**: a describing word
>
> **verb**: a doing word

Of course, the examiner does not want you to just find significant words. You also have to analyse the effect of the language used.

Mark scheme

Grade	Descriptors
7, 8, 9	● Analyses the effects of the words used ● Selects a range of quotations, exactly the right ones to use ● Uses all the correct subject terminology
5, 6	● Explains clearly the effects of the words used ● Uses a range of quotations that are relevant ● Uses subject terminology
3, 4	● Tries to comment on the words used ● Uses some relevant quotations ● Uses some subject terminology, but it is not always appropriate
1, 2	● Able to say simple things about the language ● Simple references to details in the source ● Some simple mention of subject terminology

This response is demonstrating Grade 9 skills in response to the question:
How has the writer used language to set the scene?

supported interpretations

terminology and effect

analysis throughout section

all technical effects interpreted

explaining effects throughout

The writer has used adjectives and verbs to give a clear picture of what Maycombe was like. Initially, the adjectives suggest it is far from exciting ('old', 'tired'): it seems worn out and past its best. Then, we picture it in bad weather: 'the streets turned to red slop'. The redness here does not suggest heat, because the noun 'slop' sounds unpleasant – in fact, there is **onomatopoeia**, as we can hear the sounds of things splashing through it. 'Grass grew' uses **alliteration**: these are grim 'gr's. The town is still suffering, because the verb 'sagged' suggests things are collapsing. (The vowel sound might also give an impression of droplets splashing down.)

Then, we have summer, and the **semantic field** stresses the heat and more unpleasantness. It begins with the word 'hotter', then there is a series of torrid images: 'a black dog suffered' – the verb indicates pain going on for some time; 'bony mules' sound worn down, old and underfed; they 'flicked flies', the alliteration of frantic 'f's sounding petulant; and the shade is 'sweltering', making it seem everybody is struggling to breath and suffering (the alliteration of 'sweltering shade' has sizzling 's' sounds). Even the men's collars 'wilted' like dead flowers. **Emotive language** is used throughout, to reveal how the town suffers.

terminology again, plus explanation

terminology and explanation

terminology and interpretations

terminology

onomatopoeia: when words capture a sound (e.g. splash, tinkle)

alliteration: when words begin with the same sound (catastrophic chasm, pretty paws)

semantic field: a group of words that have a relationship, creating an overall impression (e.g. passion, affection, adoration, heart – semantic field: 'love')

emotive language: words that affect our emotions

Assessment comment

This analyses the effects of the words used, selects the right quotations throughout and uses all the correct subject terminology.

Considering the examples picked out in the response, make sure you understand all the technical terms used.

Getting it right: Metaphors and similes

Read this short description. It relies heavily on **metaphors** for its effect:

> He was a small sour apple of a man, grey-skinned and shrivelled, with a dozen or so surviving strands of black hair pasted across the dome of his bald head.

Roald Dahl, Claud's Dog, 1953

metaphor: something which is not literally true

This is what a Grade 5 student wrote about the language:

> The man is not really 'a sour apple', so this is a metaphor. It means he was always miserable. He was probably not 'shrivelled' either, but it gives the impression that he was shrinking. When it says the few strands of hair were pasted across his head, this is also metaphorical – they just looked silly, as if they were stuck there. His head did not have a dome either, but maybe he looked like the top of a cathedral.

Assessment comment

This response explains clearly the effects of the metaphors used and uses relevant quotations.

This is a Grade 9 response:

> The writer is using metaphorical language throughout. The man is made to seem like a very unpleasant apple. He is 'sour', which suggests no one likes him and he leaves a bad taste in the mouth. A sour apple is not something you would want anything to do with. His skin might well have been 'grey coloured' (which sounds very unhealthy) but when he is described as 'shrivelled', this is like an old apple that is past its time and nobody wants and which needs to be thrown away. The alliteration of 'surviving strands' makes them sound like stray 's's, as if there aren't many; and they looked 'pasted' – as if they need to be stuck down, to stop them flying up in the breeze, or as if they aren't actually real. Finally, there is the metaphorical 'dome of his bald head', which does not make him sound holy, like a church, but makes the reader think the top of his head is shiny and visible from a long way away and perhaps looks too big for the man under it.

Tasks

1 Write a list of exactly what makes the second response so much better.
2 How well does it fulfil the descriptors for a Grade 9 (see page 15)?

simile: a comparison using 'like' or 'as'

Similes also add meaning and allow the reader to interpret them in different ways.

This is from a horror story called 'The Birds'. A man is on the beach when he notices the seagulls:

> They rose and fell in the trough of the seas, heads to the wind, like a mighty fleet at anchor, waiting on the tide. To eastward, and to the west, the gulls were there. They stretched as far as the eye could reach, in close formation, line upon line. Had the sea been still, they would have covered the bay like a white shroud …

Daphne du Maurier, The Birds, in The Birds and Other Stories, 1952

There are two similes here: 'like a mighty fleet at anchor' and 'like a white shroud'.

Typical mistake

Many students think it is sufficient to just identify the techniques being used (metaphors, similes, etc). However, to do well, you need to explain the effects. The more explanation about their effects you can offer, the more marks you will receive.

Task

1 Add extra explanations to these sentences:

○ The writer uses a simile when she states that the gulls were 'like a mighty fleet at anchor'. This suggests there were many of them, but also …

(Hints: Think about what the purpose of a mighty fleet might be – and what effect it might have on the enemy. Why is the term 'mighty fleet' particularly appropriate here?)

○ When the writer goes on to say that the birds 'covered the bay like a white shroud', the simile suggests that they were the only colour apparent – so the blue or grey of the sea could no longer be seen. However, by saying they covered the water 'like a white shroud' this also gives the impression that …

(Hint: Think about shrouds and where they are used and what they make us think of. Think about what this is suggesting about what might happen in the story …)

> **Exam tip**
>
> All similes and metaphors can be interpreted in more than one way. If you can find some in the section of the source you are writing about in the exam, you have the opportunity to offer more than one interpretation of them, which means you are 'analysing' – and more marks will be awarded.

Getting it right: Sentences

REVISED

You might well be dealing with four types of sentence:

- simple sentences – with just one idea or clause (e.g. I am going to the sports centre.)
- compound sentences – made up of two or more main clauses and usually joined by 'and', 'but', 'or' (e.g. I am going to the sports centre but I won't be swimming.)
- complex sentences – made up of a main clause and at least one dependent clause which would not make sense on its own

(e.g. Because I'm bored, ◀——————— dependent clause
I am going to the sports centre, ◀——————— main clause
which is just down the road.) ◀——————— dependent clause

- minor sentences – not grammatically complete: have a capital letter and punctuation to end them, but do not have a verb (e.g. So much for happiness!).

There will probably be a mix of long and short sentences, and possibly an exclamation, question, list or a sentence ending in an **ellipsis**, all of which create effects that you need to explain.

> **ellipsis**: the omission of a word or several words, which are replaced by three dots

Tasks

1 Read this text and the annotations.

first word of sentence introduces danger/worry →

Wary, not actually expecting trouble but prepared for it, he parked the car across the street from the four-storey brownstone apartment house. When he switched off the engine, he heard a siren wail in the street behind him.

← complex sentence opens with emphasis on idea trouble might come but he's prepared

They're coming for me, he thought. Somehow they've found out I'm the one.

← his simple thoughts

simple sentence registers his attitude →

He smiled. He wouldn't let them put the handcuffs on him. He wouldn't go easily.

← short sentences demonstrate his simple but complete determination

Dean R Koontz, *The Face of Fear*, 1977

2 Now read this extract and try to decide how the sentences have been used to show Eva's feelings.

Eva sat in the kitchen and looked at the clock again. It was five o'clock in the morning and she had been up since two, indulging herself in the luxury of many emotions. Her first reaction when going to bed had been one of annoyance. Then she had lain awake getting angrier and angrier by the minute until one o'clock when worry had taken over. It wasn't like Henry to stay out late. Perhaps something had happened to him. He'd had an accident with the car too and while at the time she had just put that down to his usual absent-mindedness, now that she came to think of it ... At that point, Eva had turned the light on and got out of bed. Something terrible had been going on and she hadn't even known it.

Tom Sharpe, *Wilt on High*, 1984

3 Any valid points will be accepted – but did you make any of the ones below?

This opens with a basic compound sentence establishing Eva's situation: 'Eva sat in the kitchen and looked at the clock again.' The next sentence adds detail, and clearly the time is vital, because it comes first ('It was five o'clock in the morning'). We now have her in a place and time; and it's a complex sentence which, perhaps, mirrors the complexity in her thoughts, her 'many emotions'.

The feelings then build ('Her first reaction ... Then ... until ...'). Her panic develops through the stages. Worry is her over-riding reaction, though, highlighted by simple statements:

'It wasn't like Henry to stay out late. Perhaps something had happened to him.'

Next, Eva's mind starts to wander and the complex sentence guides us through her various thoughts about the accident; and ends with an ellipsis, because she is so worried she doesn't want to develop that line of thought any further or maybe what would follow is obvious ...

Assessment comment

Thus far, the response analyses the effects of the sentences used, selects exactly the right quotations and uses correct subject terminology. It is in the top band of marks.

4 Write about the final two sentences in a similarly analytical way.

Test yourself

In this extract, how does the writer use language to show Adam's state of mind?

You could write about:
- words and phrases
- language features and techniques
- sentence forms.

It was Adam Appleby's misfortune that at the moment of awakening from sleep his consciousness was immediately flooded with everything he least wanted to think about. Other men, he gathered, met each new dawn with a refreshed mind and heart, full of optimism; or else they moved sluggishly through the first hour of the day in a state of blessed numbness, incapable of any thought at all, pleasant or unpleasant. But, crouched like evil spirits around his bed, unpleasant thoughts waited to pounce the moment Adam's eyelids flickered apart. At that moment, he was forced, like a drowning man, to review his entire life, divided between regrets for the past and fears for the future.

David Lodge, *The British Museum is falling down*

How to prepare for the exam

Find sections of stories about ten lines long and list or underline all the language features you could comment on.
At the side, jot annotations indicating what you would say about the language.
Repeat as often as possible!

Paper 1, Q3 Dealing with structure

What this question involves

You will be asked about how the fiction source has been structured. You might write about:

- the opening
- how the ideas develop or change
- other structural features in the source.

Timing

You will already have read the source(s).

There are 8 marks for this question, which you will need to complete in 8 or 9 minutes.

What the examiner is looking for

The examiner is hoping you show detailed and perceptive understanding of the structure and:

- analyse the effects of how the writer structures the text
- use the best examples to support what you say
- use subject terminology well.

In this unit you will revise:

how to write about:

- narrative perspective
- openings
- developments
- other structural features.

Getting it right: Narrative perspective

REVISED ☐

Read this extract in which the writer describes a past girlfriend:

> Penny Hardwick was a nice girl, and, nowadays, I'm all for nice girls, although then I wasn't so sure. She had a nice mum and dad, and a nice house, detached, with a garden and a tree and a fishpond, and a nice girl's haircut (she was blonde, and she kept her hair a sort of clean, wholesome, form-captain mid-length) and nice, smiling eyes, and a nice younger sister …
>
> Nick Hornby, *High Fidelity*, 1995

Task

1 Next you can read part of a Grade 7 response to the question: How does this writer use **narrative perspective?**

> **narrative perspective**: the viewpoint from which the story is told
>
> **first person**: told from the viewpoint of someone involved in the story

The story is told from a **first-person** perspective (he says, 'I wasn't so sure'), so we only know what the narrator is thinking. The second sentence is really long, because he presents his ideas about Penny as he remembers them, and one idea seems to tumble into another. Also, of course, we hear the narrator's voice throughout (hence the repetition of 'nice').

supporting quotation

appropriate terminology

effect of the structure

supported comment

Task

1 Read this extract from an **omniscient narrator** and, with the previous approach in mind, write one or two sentences explaining how this story is being told.

In the morning, the little Mexican left the house at seven o'clock alone, hurrying down the alley, observing the same silence he kept in his rooms. She followed at eight o'clock, walking carefully, all lumpy under her dark coat, a black hat balanced on her frizzy, beauty parlour hair. They had gone to work this way, remote and silent, for years.

Ray Bradbury, *The Day It Rained Forever*, 1957

> **omniscient narrator**: the person telling the story knows everything
>
> Sometimes there is a third-person narrator (a person looking down on the story) who is not omniscient: the writer just follows one character, only saying what they do and say and think.

Getting it right: Openings

REVISED ☐

The first few lines are always intended to have an effect on the reader. They are an essential part of the structure.

Tasks

1 Read this opening and decide whether the story that follows is likely to be happy or sad. How do you know?

Now in the autumn the trees were all bare and the roads were muddy. I rode to Gorizia from Udine on a lorry. We passed other lorries on the road and I looked at the country. The mulberry trees were bare and the fields were brown. There were wet dead leaves on the road from the rows of bare trees ...

Hopefully, you noticed the effect of the details (bare, muddy, brown, wet, dead) and interpreted their effect.

2 Decide what this opening is suggesting about the story to come.

There are women whose eyes lock momentarily in bars, across crowded rooms, in the street and, though they are strangers, they recognise each other. They go through that female summing up thing, the quick look from toes to haircut, and for a second their eyes meet.

When Cora O'Brien's eyes met Ellen Quinn's across the crowded living room at one of Jack Conroy's parties, Ellen thought: Who is that vividly dressed woman? And Cora thought: I could be friends with you!

Isla Dewar, *Women Talking Dirty*, 1996

This is just part of a Grade 4 response to the task.

> This opening tells us that the story will be about Cora O'Brien and Ellen Quinn. It will be a story for girls because it is about what women do: 'that female summing up thing'. It talks about how they decide about people by giving them 'the quick look from toes to haircut'.

Consider the mark scheme for this question and decide what more the candidate might do to improve the grade.

Grade	Descriptors
7, 8, 9	• Extremely detailed response which shows clever understanding of the structure • Analyses the effects of the structural features • Selects a range of quotations, exactly the right ones to use • Uses all the correct subject terminology
5, 6	• Clearly understands the structure • Explains clearly the effects of the structural features • Uses a range of quotations that are relevant • Uses subject terminology
3, 4	• There is some understanding of the structure • Tries to comment on the structure • Uses some relevant quotations • Uses some subject terminology, but it is not always appropriate
1, 2	• Just aware of some structural features • Able to say simple things about the structure and its effect • Simple references to details in the source • Some simple mention of subject terminology

Getting it right: How ideas develop or change

REVISED

This is the opening of a book set in the future, where everyone is watched. 'Barbieheart' is on a screen in the house, monitoring the family.

Trafford said goodbye to his wife, kissed their tiny baby on the forehead and began to unlock the various bolts and deadlocks that secured their front door.

respectful → 'And a very good morning to you too, Trafford,' said the voice of Barbieheart. ← sarcasm?

'Yes, of course, good morning, Barbieheart,' Trafford replied nervously. 'Good morning indeed, I mean goodbye ... I mean ... well, I mean I don't want to be late, you see.' ← he is uneasy / nervousness revealed

telling him she is not to blame → 'I'm not holding you up, Trafford.'

he doesn't argue with her → 'No. Absolutely.'

'Well now, you take care to have a great day.' ← genuine good wishes – or a command?

'Thank you. Thank you very much. I will.' ← seems afraid – or very respectful

Trafford's wife looked at him angrily. He knew she suspected him of deliberately not greeting Barbieheart, as some kind of protest, some bizarre bid for independence. She was right, of course. ← we learn his actual state of mind

Ben Elton, *Blind Faith*, 2007

The relationship between Trafford and Barbieheart is gradually exposed in this extract. Writing about the development, you might mention the points in the annotations.

Question: **Write an explanation of how the writer develops the relationship between Trafford and Barbieheart.**

Tasks

1 This is just part of a response to the question.
   Can you spot the Grade 9 qualities?

> The 'various bolts and deadlocks' suggest there is something
> strange or frightening about this place – but we then get the voice of
> Barbieheart: 'And a very good morning to you *too*, Trafford.' The name
> suggests someone pretty and cuddly, but she is obviously offended
> and there is sarcasm in her tone. There is a development, though,
> because we realise that she might be part of the problem: although he
> is in his own house, Trafford is overly respectful towards her ('Yes, of
> course, good morning'); and he 'replied nervously'. This is an unusual
> situation and the way you might react to someone in charge.

2 Complete the analysis, examining how the scene develops. Include
   some of the remaining annotated quotations.

In this opening, the ideas move on rapidly.

> My fascinating life.
>
> Yes.
>
> Born March 20th, 1977, in Bradford, Yorkshire to Mr and Mrs X. We
> were a family, you know – as happy as most, till Dad ran off with a
> receptionist in 1991, when I was fourteen and at the local school.
> This mucked up my school work for a while, but that's not why I
> ended up like this. No, Vincent's to blame for that. Good old Vince.
> Mum's boyfriend. You should see him. I mean, Mum's no Kylie
> Minogue – but Vincent. He's about fifty for a start, and he's one
> of those old dudes that wear cool gear and try to act young and it
> doesn't work because they've got grey hair and fat bellies and they
> just make themselves pathetic.

Robert Swindells, Stone Cold, 1993

If you were writing about how this is structured, you might deal with:
- how the positive opening is presented through the brief ideas/
  paragraphs
- how basic biographical details move into more personal memories in
  the much longer paragraph
- how the narrator introduces three characters rapidly, but dwells on
  Vincent
- how the sense of a speaking voice is maintained.

3 Write your answer to this question:
   How is this opening structured to engage the reader?

Exam tip

Always remember what
question you are answering.
In this case, you are writing
about *how* the scene
develops so the relationship
is gradually revealed, not
just what the relationship is
like. You need to be focusing
on how the writer introduces
the developments.

Getting it right: Other structural features

REVISED

Writers might use techniques such as:

- a short paragraph to stress a point
- a movement from a general viewpoint to more specific details
- long descriptive sentences contrasting with sudden shorter, dramatic ones
- speech to indicate character or to move the story along
- repetition for emphasis
- narrative that shifts from place to place
- a motif — a repeated mention of, for example, stars and the galaxy, to remind us of how insignificant mankind is; or of water, making us think of growth and rebirth
- movement between times (for example, the past and present)
- contrasts: for example, in people or settings.

Read this opening to a novel.

> High atop the steps of the Great Pyramid of Giza a young woman laughed and called down to him. 'Robert, hurry up! I knew I should have married a younger man!' Her smile was magic.
>
> He struggled to keep up, but his legs felt like stone. 'Wait,' he begged. 'Please …'
>
> As he climbed, his vision began to blur. There was a thundering in his ears. *I must reach her!* But when he looked up again, the woman had disappeared. In her place stood an old man with rotting teeth. The man stared down, curling his lips into a lonely grimace. Then he let out a scream of anguish that resounded across the desert.
>
> Robert Langdon woke with a start from his nightmare. The phone beside his bed was ringing.

Dan Brown, *Angels and Demons*, 2000

Here is part of a Grade 9 analysis of how the structure works.

immediate understanding of writer's method

extends the idea

analysing: linked ideas

understands how the text works

> The short paragraphs give the whole extract a sense of excitement; it feels as if there is much happening and it is all very rapid. In fact, we are introduced to an apparently dangerous situation right at the start ('High atop …'). The speech then moves the drama along, though once more speed is paramount: 'Robert, hurry up!' There is no actual tension at this point, because we have humour, as if all will be well: 'I should have married a younger man!' – and also, 'her smile was magic', which sounds wonderful. Of course, though, in the light of what happens next, we wonder whether this is actually a positive or whether we are being introduced to black magic.
>
> In fact, all is not well for the man. The short paragraph presents very simply his apparently desperate situation, the words contrasting with her joyfulness : 'struggled', 'legs felt like stone', 'begged', 'Wait … Please.'

exactly the right quotations throughout

structure appreciated

technique identified

analysis again; effect on reader

appreciation of structure

Task

1 Continue this analysis. You might want to write about:

○ the short sentences

○ his thought (in italics)

○ 'curling his lips' (contrasting with her smile earlier)

○ the switch in location and mood.

Test yourself

This is from the opening of a novel. How has the writer structured it to interest you as a reader?

You could write about:

● what the writer focuses your attention on at the beginning

● how and why this focus changes

● any other structural features that interest you.

On Tuesday Nan phoned Roz with details of her funeral.

'I've been to the undertaker's. Got a coffin. Plain pine. I don't know. Undertakers.' Ashe breathed out frustration. She hated not getting what she wanted. 'Dour lot. Why can't they do a nice box in pink? Or red? Stripes, maybe. Or tartan? Such a price for a boring lump of wood you're going to burn anyway.'

Not really registering what she was hearing, Roz pointed out that such coffins *were* available these days.

'Where?' asked Nan, affronted. 'Not at my undertaker's. Anyway, I've chose my songs. I want a bit of Bob Marley. None of your "Oh Perfect Love". That stuff. I want a good tune. A bit of toe-tapping.'

Roz pulled the receiver from her ear, considered it. She didn't like the sound of this. But, Nan. You never knew what Nan was going to come up with next. A few weeks ago she's spent a bit of time trying to get on a TV quiz show. But this? This time she'd gone too far. 'For God's sake, Nan. There's no need for all that. You're not going to die. Not for ages and ages.'

'Rubbish,' said Nan. 'I'm old.'

The times Nan had said that. For the past ten years, she'd phoned Roz, in London, Crouch End, at least twice weekly from her house in a long grey Edinburgh terrace. Every time she'd remarked on her great age. This time it was different. For the first time, Roz realised, Nan hadn't been telling her about her ancientness. She's been telling herself. Reminding herself. Coming to terms with it.

'I'm old,' Nan repeated firmly. 'Old. That's what happens. It sneaks up on you – age. You get born, you live, you do the things you do. Then you snuff it. I've done the things I've done. Death's the next thing. It's time to get things sorted. I've not got long.'

Isla Dewar, *Two Kinds of Wonderful*, 2000

How to prepare for the exam

Read the opening section of a story.

Taking just 8 or 9 minutes, write about how it has been structured to interest the reader.

As with any other skill, the more you practise, the better you will become.

Paper 1, Q4 Character, relationships, themes and settings

What this question involves

You will be asked about some elements of the fiction source – possibly characters, relationships, themes or settings.

In addition, you will have to evaluate the impressions created – say how successfully they have been presented.

Timing

You will already have read the source.

There are 20 marks for this question, which you will need to complete it in 20 or 21 minutes.

What the examiner is looking for

The examiner is hoping you will:
● assess how well the source has been written
● offer convincing evidence for your views
● analyse the writer's methods and their effects
● use the best examples, to support what you say.

In this unit you will revise:

● impressions created in texts
● how to deal with the effects created by writers' methods
● how to evaluate the writers' success.

Throughout, ideas will have to be supported with evidence.

Getting it right: Impressions of character

REVISED ☐

Shahid has been sacked from his tailoring job and been replaced by Rasul. What impression of Shahid do we get here?

> Whenever Shahid got angry his short cropped hair seemed to stand up of his head. Like the feathers on the neck of a fighting cock. He was very angry that day. When the four of us left the factory and reached the street, he said we should go straight to his uncle's house.
>
> 'He will deal with the guv'nor,' Shahid said. 'I will show that Rasul. Son of a hired woman. When he comes out of the factory I will see him.'
>
> Farrukh Dhondy, *Come to Mecca*, 1978

Tasks

1 What do each of the following quotations suggest about Shahid?
   ○ 'Whenever Shahid got angry'
   ○ 'Like the feathers on the neck of a fighting cock'
   ○ 'he said we should go straight to his uncle's house'
   ○ 'Son of a hired woman'
   ○ 'When he comes out of the factory I will see him'

2 Complete this response, saying what impression we get of Shahid.

> Shahid appears to be hot-headed. It is not just that he is angry at this point in the story – it obviously happens often ('Whenever Shahid got angry ...'). In fact, it is as if he had been born to fight, because ...

— impression created

— interpreting

Shahid and his friends meet a girl and go round to where she lives.

> We went the next day. We sat on the floor in her strange room. She didn't even have a settee, and her bed was just one mattress on the floor, like a villager. There were hundreds of books all over the place. Everyone who came to her room sat on the floor on cushions amongst all the books and tea-mugs and papers. Even the light was hanging down from the ceiling nearly to the floor with a paper bowl on it, and there were coloured candles which had spread pools of wax on the furniture.
>
> She told us that she was a translator and showed us some Russian books and French books and Shahid asked her to say something in French and in Russian, and she said it and we all laughed. When he asked her what that meant, she said, 'It means "I love you"' and we all laughed again, and she could see that Shahid thought she was saying it to him, so she said, 'It's the easiest thing to say in any language.'

Farrukh Dhondy, *Come to Mecca*, 1978

3 What impression of the girl do we get here? In your answer, mention:
- ○ what the room tells us about her
- ○ her job
- ○ how the extract ends.

Getting it right: Impressions of relationships

`REVISED`

Rasul, who has taken Shahid's job, was prepared to work for less money. This is a flashback to what happened when he arrived.

> 'So, you've come to put your foot on my stomach, eh, Rasul?' Shahid challenged.
>
> Rasul sheepishly picked up the cloth that Shahid had been working at and started to put it through the machine.
>
> 'Don't talk so big when you're only a chit of a boy,' Rasul replied.
>
> 'I have more pride in my chin than you have in your white beard. Only orphans work for fifty pence,' Shahid said.
>
> 'I work for what I can get. When you have three children you'll stop going to the pub with your money and going with white girls,' Rasul said, still working away.

Farrukh Dhondy, *Come to Mecca*, 1978

Tasks

1 Put the following statements into two lists, deciding which of them best suit each character and their attitude to the other.

Shahid	Rasul

○ He thinks … is supporting the gaffer against him.
○ He thinks … is prepared to challenge him.
○ He thinks … is embarrassed.
○ He is dismissive of … and his attitude.
○ He implies … should expect more money.
○ He thinks … would have a different attitude if he had a family.
○ He thinks … has a bad lifestyle.

2 Use the lists you have created to show what we learn about their relationship. Include:
○ Shahid's attitude to Rasul
○ Rasul's attitude to Shahid.

Exam tip

Remember to say how an impression is created and support your comment with reference to how the writer gives you that the impression, e.g. "Rasul does not like being spoken to in an insulting way by Shahid and so he insults him in return, calling him 'a chit of a boy'."

Getting it right: Impressions of theme

REVISED ☐

Task

1 Decide what the theme in this extract is.

The story is told by an Etruscan hostage, who has been captured by the Romans during the fourth century BC. The Romans, however, are besieged in a walled town and are trying to destroy the morale of the Etruscans surrounding them.

> There were only three of us left now; the others had been hung over the ramparts, one every morning. Elxsente was still sick and we didn't know what to do with him; he was only a child, and cried for his mother at nights; some of the others had done that, and I would have too, but I was fifteen and had to set a good example. They used to take us out on to the walls, and whip us where the men from our Cities could see us; of course they had the right to do it, but some of us weren't very old, and used to cry even at the thought of it, which was bad for everyone. But we could look out when we were taken up, and there was our camp, spread and shining below us; once there was an attack while we were there and we all cheered, but the Romans paid us back in kicks for that. Every day we hoped the town would fall, though we should very likely have been killed before anyone could get to us; still, it was better than being dragged out and choked like dogs at the end of a rope.

Naomi Mitchison, *The Hostages*, 1930

A Grade 4 student decided the theme was 'the cruelty of war'. Asked about how the impression of war was created, this is what he wrote:

an example to explain view →

quotation supporting the view →

> The writer shows that war is bad. Some hostages have been hung and Elxsente was 'only a child' and cried for his mother. The Romans were horrible to them and whipped them and made them cry, so it shows that war was grim: 'which was bad for everyone'. They could have been 'choked like dogs at the end of a rope'.

← simple comment on writer's method

← simple example

This is the mark scheme for Question 4.

Grade	Descriptors
7, 8, 9	● Evaluates the text critically and in detail ● Chooses convincing examples to explain views ● Analyses the effects of some of the writer's methods ● Selects a range of quotations, exactly the right ones to use
5, 6	● Evaluates the text clearly ● Chooses examples to explain views clearly ● Explains clearly the effects of some of the writer's methods ● Uses a range of quotations that are relevant
3, 4	● Tries to evaluate the text ● Uses example(s) from the text to explain view(s) ● Tries to comment on the writer's methods ● Uses some relevant quotations
1, 2	● Comments in a simple way on the text ● Chooses simple examples from the text which might explain view(s) ● Able to say simple things about the writer's method(s) ● Simple references to details in the source

Task

1 Without worrying about evaluation at this point, write a better explanation of how war is presented in the text. Go into more precise detail. Offer more supported explanation of what it makes you think about war.

Getting it right: Impressions of settings

REVISED

This is how the Etruscan narrator describes his arrival in Rome, in chains.

At first there was nothing but choking dust, until we got to the suburbs, where the streets had been watered, which kept the dust down and was pleasant to the feet. But then the crowds began, crowds of shouting enemies on the two edges of the road; they frightened me more than anything; we were so helpless and alone in the middle of them, and sometimes the noise would suddenly swell up into a roar all round us, and Elxsente would shrink up close to me; once or twice they threw things at us, but nothing sharp enough to cut. A man who walked in front of us kept on repeating in a shout that we were the hostages from the Cities who were spared by order of the General and that the rest were hung. He said it over and over again like a corncrake: I would have given a lot to kill that man.

Naomi Mitchison, *The Hostages*, 1930

Consider this question: **What impression of their arrival is presented here and what methods does the writer use to make it vivid?**

You might decide to
- give an **overview** of the scene; then
- select methods the writer uses, giving examples and quotations to support and develop your impression.

> overview: a summary of the content or what happens in the text

Using this approach, a Grade 6 student began like this.

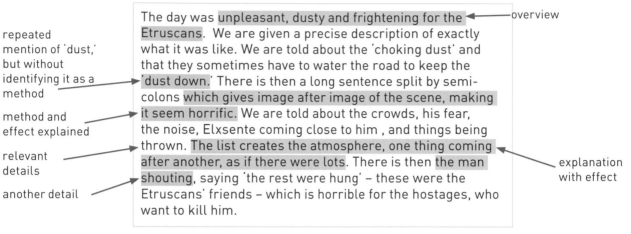

repeated mention of 'dust,' but without identifying it as a method

method and effect explained

relevant details

another detail

The day was unpleasant, dusty and frightening for the Etruscans. We are given a precise description of exactly what it was like. We are told about the 'choking dust' and that they sometimes have to water the road to keep the 'dust down.' There is then a long sentence split by semi-colons which gives image after image of the scene, making it seem horrific. We are told about the crowds, his fear, the noise, Elxsente coming close to him, and things being thrown. The list creates the atmosphere, one thing coming after another, as if there were lots. There is then the man shouting, saying 'the rest were hung' – these were the Etruscans' friends – which is horrible for the hostages, who want to kill him.

overview

explanation with effect

Study the annotations and assessment comment, then read the following extract and respond to the tasks.

In this extract, there is a party in a rich man's mansion near New York in the 1920s.

> **Assessment comment**
>
> This uses examples, explains some effects and has relevant quotations to support the points being made.

> We walked through a high hallway into a bright rosy-coloured space, fragilely bound into the house by French windows at either end. The windows were ajar and gleaming white against the fresh grass outside that seemed to grow a little way into the house. A breeze blew through the room, blew curtains in at one end and out the other like pale flags, twisting them up toward the frosted wedding cake of the ceiling, and then rippled over the wine-coloured rug, making a shadow on it as wind does on the sea.
>
> The only completely stationary object in the room was an enormous couch on which two young women were buoyed up as though upon an anchored balloon. They were both in white, and their dresses were rippling and fluttering as if they had just been blown back in after a short flight around the house.
>
> F Scott Fitzgerald, *The Great Gatsby*, 1925

Tasks

1 Write a sentence giving an overview of the setting.
2 Decide what the effect is of each of the following:
   - 'bright rosy-coloured space'
   - 'fragilely bound into the house'
   - 'The windows were … gleaming white'
   - 'the fresh grass … seemed to grow a little way into the house'
   - 'A breeze … blew curtains … like pale flags'
   - 'frosted wedding cake of a ceiling'
   - 'rippled over the wine coloured rug'

- ○ 'making a shadow on it as wind does on the sea'
- ○ 'two young women were buoyed up as though upon an anchored balloon'
- ○ 'their dresses were rippling and fluttering as if they had been blown back in …'

In the exam, you would probably not be able to deal with all these images, but would have the time to write in detail about some of them.

Here is a question on the whole extract:

How does the writer present a clear picture of the setting in this text?

You should:

- write about your own impression of the setting
- support your opinions with quotations from the text.

A Grade 2 student wrote:

simple opening

simple mention of method

selects suitable quotation

> The writer tries to give a clear picture by telling us what it is like. He gives us lots of different details about the windows and the grass and the ceiling and the two women looking as if they have just been blown in. This makes it all stand out so we can think what it is like in our heads. It is a 'bright rosy-coloured space' so the writer is saying it must have bright lights on and some of the paint is red to make it rosy.

simple mention of method

examples to support idea

simple comment on writers' method

Task

1 Write your own answer to the question:

- giving an overview
- explaining how the writer presents a clear picture, through precise reference to the writer's methods, including:
  - ○ analysis of the effects of some of the images used
  - ○ how details build together to give an overall impression.

Getting it right: Analysing and evaluating the writer's methods

REVISED

Paper 1, Question 4 is different from the other questions because you are expected to **evaluate** the text. That means you have to say how well the text has been written.

evaluate: judge the success of something

You are likely to need a set of phrases which help you fulfil the requirement, such as:

- This clearly shows that …
- The writer has managed to …
- This works well, because …
- We are able to understand that …
- Obviously, … therefore, …
- Here the words successfully highlight …
- The reader is bound to think …
- We know immediately that …

As part of the evaluation, the question is likely to ask you for your reactions to the text and what it has made you think.

As in Questions 2 and 3, if you can analyse – offer different interpretations – you will be heading towards the top marks.

So, for example, if you were asked about how successfully the writer presents the scene of the party in *The Great Gatsby* (see p.30), a Grade 9 response might begin:

The writer presents the scene clearly by focusing on small elements which give us an impression of what it must have been like: light and beautiful. The images work effectively because we understand what they are suggesting. So, when we read about 'the frosted wedding cake of the ceiling', we think of its whiteness and imagine it might have been built originally for a celebration and fits well with the current party; and, if it is 'frosted', the writer does not just imply it is white, but also, perhaps, has managed to suggest that there is something frozen, as if there is no real life or warmth in the room …

Annotations:
- initial evaluation
- clear overview to introduce the analysis
- evaluates again
- alternative interpretations: analysis
- evaluation of writer's success
- alternatives (analysis) again

Task

1 Choose two details from the text that you did not include in your earlier answer and write about them now, ensuring you include:
   ○ analysis of their effects
   ○ evaluation of how successfully the writer has described the scene.

Read the extract below. This story is set in the outback of Australia in the 1850s, when the first white settlers were moving inland. A woman and her husband, John, have started a ranch and employ Aborigines – native Australians; here, we are shown some attitudes towards them.

> She didn't like Lloyd. She had told John so, many a time. But her husband just said that men were difficult to get; Lloyd was all right, a good stockman and all that. But she didn't trust the fellow; he was altogether too rough on the natives. John himself could be brutal enough at times, but he was always just; the boys respected the boss, liked him – his kind of brutality was their own, and seen only when the isolation of the place rendered a firm hand advisable. But that Lloyd! She could never forget seeing him set the dogs on the Aborigine women one day, so the poor wretches ran screaming to the trees and scaled them like cats. Horrible, it had been. And Lloyd had laughed fit to kill himself. Pity he hadn't! She had told John. That time he had spoken to the man, said such a thing must not happen again. And it hadn't.

H Drake Brockman, *Fear*

Question: **What impression do you get of the characters here?**

Tasks

1 Make a list of points and supporting quotations about each of the characters, e.g.

The narrator:
1 dislikes Lloyd – 'she didn't like Lloyd' ...
2 ...

Lloyd:
1 Seems to work well – 'a good stockman and all that' ...
2 ...

John:
1 Has a hard side to his nature – 'could be brutal enough at times' ...
2 ...

This is how a Grade 8 student began a full answer.

The writer intends us to dislike Lloyd, right from the start. Because we know the narrator 'didn't like Lloyd' and the story is being told through her eyes, we are intended to feel the same way about him. When she exclaims 'But that Lloyd', we cannot fail to feel her emotion; and when she gives the example of how he set the dogs on the women, we are appalled, as the writer expects. They are described as 'poor wretches' which gives us an image of them in rags and suffering, but also puts the actions of Lloyd into perspective, so we dislike him all the more.

writer's purpose

effect and evaluation

impression created

evaluating

analysing effect

2 Write a full answer of your own. In your answer, try to:
- ○ write about your impressions of the characters
- ○ evaluate how the writer has created these impressions
- ○ support your opinions with quotations from the extract.

Test yourself

Will has gone to visit Christine and John, who have a new baby, Imogen.

Christine came in holding the new baby while John was in the kitchen making him a cup of tea. 'This is Imogen,' she said.

'Oh,' said Will. 'Right.' What was he supposed to say next? He knew there was something, but he couldn't for the life of him remember what it was. 'She's …' No. It had gone. He concentrated his conversational efforts on Christine. 'How are you, anyway, Chris?'

'Oh, you know. A bit washed out.'

'Been burning the candle at both ends?'

'No, just had a baby.'

'Oh. Right.' Everything came back to the sodding baby. 'That would make you pretty tired, I guess.' He'd deliberately waited a week so that he wouldn't have to talk about this sort of thing, but it hadn't done him any good. They were talking about it anyway.

John came in with a tray and three mugs of tea.

'Barney's gone to his grandma's today,' he said, for no reason at all that Will could see.

'How is Barney?' Barney was two, that was how Barney was, and therefore of no interest to anyone apart from his parents, but, again, for reasons he would never fathom, some comment seemed to be required of him.

'He's fine, thanks,' said John. 'He's a right little devil at the moment, mind you, and he's not too sure what to make of Imogen, but … he's lovely.'

Will had met Barney before, and knew for a fact he wasn't lovely.

Nick Hornby, *About a Boy*, 1998

Having read this extract, a student wrote: 'These are just like real people.'

To what extent do you agree?

In your response, you should:
- write about your impression of these characters
- evaluate how the writer has created these impressions
- support what you say with quotations.

How to prepare for the exam

You need practice in analysing and evaluating.

Read short extracts and think:
- **Analysis:** 'Could I interpret what is said, what happens, the images or the writer's methods in more than one way? What would I say?'
- **Evaluation:** 'How could I add evaluation to my ideas?' Practise using evaluative phrases as you consider the effectiveness of the writing (see the examples on p. 31).

Exam tip

You have at least 20 minutes to answer this question. That allows you enough time to jot down some rapid notes before you begin, so you remember to include those points.

What does Paper 2, Section A involve?

What you have to do ...

Paper 2, Section A is challenging because you have to deal with two texts on a similar subject – one from the nineteenth century and one from the twentieth or twenty-first century. They will be non-fiction, so they might be diary entries, letters, articles, biography or reports.

It is especially important that you do not panic about the nineteenth-century extract. Even if some of the language or ideas are tricky, read slowly and carefully and it will begin to make sense.

As with Paper 1, Section A, there are 40 marks available.

You are advised to spend approximately 1 hour on the section, reading the texts and answering the questions. If you commit approximately 15 minutes to reading the texts carefully, that will leave you 45 minutes to write your answers.

The questions will be as follows:

Q1	4 marks	You will be given 8 statements about one of the texts: you have to shade in boxes to say which 4 are true.
Q2	8 marks	You will need to write about both texts and summarise some element of their differences or similarities.
Q3	12 marks	Focusing on just one of the texts, you will have to say how the writer has used language for effect.
Q4	16 marks	You have to consider both texts again and this time compare their ideas or attitudes – for example, the attitude of the writers towards a person or a place – but you also compare the methods they use to present their ideas and attitudes.

As with Paper 1, if you have spent 15 minutes reading the texts, you know how long to spend writing your answers. So, for example, the 12-mark question will need to be completed in 12 or 13 minutes – or in 14 minutes, perhaps, if you have managed to read the texts quickly.

Once again, there are no marks for your technical accuracy, but you should try to be as accurate as possible, to help the examiner understand what you are saying. If the examiners find your English is confused or confusing, or if they can't read your handwriting, it is difficult for them to reward you highly.

Paper 2, Q1 Finding what is true

What this question involves

You will be presented with 8 statements about the opening section of one of the non-fiction sources.

You will have to shade in boxes to indicate which 4 statements are true.

Timing

You will already have read the source.

There are 4 marks for this question, which you will need to complete in about 4 minutes.

What the examiner is looking for

There will be 1 mark for each correct identification you make.

In this unit you will revise:

● finding **explicit** information
● finding **implicit** information.

Read this text, about sports fanatics.

> The thing is, they are so limited in their outlook. They don't think about life and what really matters: the state of the country, the state of the world – even their own family sometimes. They just live for the weekend and the next match or the next awayday to some far-flung outpost of sporting mediocrity.
>
> My brother is a Huddersfield Town fan. (Please don't laugh, he has suffered mockery throughout his life.) This means he has lived in a dream world for years, and he really believes that his team is destined for greatness and has a history to be proud of. That is lunacy. Worse still, he spends a fortune to watch them lose and fail and be humiliated. Maybe he deserves sympathy, or medical attention, but we should also ask why he feels the need for escapism and fantasy. Was it his education that caused the defects?
>
> Of course, he is not alone. Some are similarly entranced by the magic of rugby, tennis, even polo, I imagine...

When you think about the statements given on the exam paper, you need to decide which are true; and it will often help to decide which are clearly incorrect.

> **explicit**: clearly stated – leaving no room for doubt
>
> **implicit**: something suggested but not clearly stated

Task

1 Which of these statements are true and which are false?

A Sports fans do not care about their families.
B All sport is mediocre.
C The writer's brother is a Huddersfield Town fan.
D Huddersfield Town are destined for greatness.
E His brother is a lunatic.
F The writer thinks perhaps we should not be too hard on the writer's brother.
G It is possible that his brother was affected by his education.
H Other sports hold a similar magic for their supporters.

Test Yourself answers at **www.hoddereducation.co.uk/myrevisionnotes/gcse-english-language**

Hopefully, you decided:

A is false. The text says 'even their own families sometimes': the final word means this does not apply to all sports fans.

B is false. The text simply says that he visits places 'of sporting mediocrity': this does not apply to all sport.

C is true. The statement comes straight from the text.

D is false. This statement is echoing his brother's hopes, and is not a statement of fact.

E is false. He claims his brother's dreams are 'lunacy' but that does not make his brother mad.

F is true. He writes 'Maybe he deserves sympathy...'

G is true. He writes: 'Was it his education that caused the defects and this is presumably 'possible'

H is true. A list of other sports is given at the end.

Getting it right: Finding explicit information

REVISED

Read this extract.

> One of the most glorious things about food is how it breaks up the day. After a rested night there's breakfast. The morning – feasibly punctuated by a cup of coffee, a bite of fruit, a biscuit even – is followed by lunch. The afternoon drifts on with a pause possibly for a cup of tea and, who knows, a stolen moment of bliss with a piece of cake. Then there is dinner. At 8pm. It all sounds simple. So straightforward. So sensible. Especially if you endeavour to eat the most at the start of the day and decrease the portions as the time moves on; better for body and soul and a good night's sleep.
>
> There was some interference with this perfect order of things a few years back when some experts, aka lunatics, suggested it would be better if you grazed all day.
>
> William Sitwell, 'A lazy, vulgar rip-off – it's time to ban brunch',
> *The Daily Telegraph*, 2014

Task

1 Which four of these points are correct? Shade in four boxes.

To get the correct answers:
○ read each statement in turn
○ read the relevant part of the text
○ decide whether the statement is true or false.

A You might have fruit during the morning. ☐
B Breakfast is soon followed by lunch. ☐
C Some people might have a cup of tea in the afternoon. ☐
D Eating cake can be a moment of bliss. ☐
E Everyone should eat lots of portions as the time moves on. ☐
F It seems sensible to have a regular pattern of eating. ☐
G You get a good night's sleep if you eat cheese. ☐
H A few years ago, mad men decided we should eat like cows. ☐

Mark scheme

You will get 1 mark for each correct selection.

The fact that some words are in the text does not mean the statement is correct. Here, for example, E includes 'lots of portions as the time moves on' but is incorrect.

Task

1 A student chose A, B, C and D, but one is incorrect. Which one and why?

Getting it right: Finding implicit information

Sometimes, you must decide whether things are true by working out what is being suggested.

Read this text.

> On February 6th, 1668, the Queen Catherine of England, wife of King Charles II, was a very unhappy woman, and like many miserable wives before and since she gave a dinner party to try to forget for an evening the neglect and unkindness of her spouse.
>
> Those were not the days when a telephone call to a first-class hotel was effort enough to produce a meal to be remembered by emperors. Every dish, flavouring and sauce had to be prepared at home, and, except for spices, lemons and oranges, to be grown at home.
>
> The storage room of an ordinary house was as big as its kitchen, which, in those days, meant as large a shelf-space as a county grocer's shop today. Imagine the tremendous stores the Royal cook must have had at his disposal, for he rarely had less than a hundred guests at the Royal table, while his under-cooks had often a thousand retainers to cater for.
>
> Jane Purves, 'The Queen's Dinner', in *The Women's Magazine Annual*, 1935

Task

1 Are the following statements true or not?

A Queen Catherine hoped to entertain her husband.
B Queen Catherine was trying to cope in an unhappy marriage.
C The writer knows about how the rich live.
D There were telephones in 1668.
E The writer is used to living in large houses.
F Royal catering took a lot of effort.
G There are always over a hundred guests at the Royal table.
H The writer has probably studied the history of the time.

> **Exam tip**
>
> Remember that only four points can be correct – and they are unlikely to be A, B, C and D.

Hopefully, you found that A, D, E and G were untrue, if you looked for implicit meanings.

Test yourself

Read this. Which four statements are true? Shade in the four boxes.

Life isn't fair, awful things happen to blameless people, but then just occasionally the universe seems to get it right. Matthew Thomas, a 38-year-old former high school teacher, is the sort of gentle, hard-working, thoughtful human for whom you wish nothing less than, well, a million-dollar book deal. A reward he won after spending a decade writing *We Are Not Ourselves*, his first novel, an epic tale of family life written in the most un-epic of circumstances.

'We were in a one-bedroom apartment,' he explains. 'The kids were in the bedroom, my wife in the bed on the other side of the room and I'd be at the kitchen table late at night trying to work under a lamp very close to the table.'

Hermione Hoby, 'I learned how to be a person writing this thing', *The New Review, The Observer*, 2014

A Matthew used to teach in high school.   ☐

B He was sacked as a teacher.   ☐

C Matthew made money by selling his book.   ☐

D The book took twenty years to write.   ☐

E The book was based on his family life.   ☐

F He disturbed the children.   ☐

G It must have been difficult to write the book.   ☐

H His wife must have been very understanding.   ☐

How to prepare for the exam

Read newspaper articles:
- What is true?
- What is being suggested?

Paper 2, Q2 Dealing with two texts and summarising

What this question involves

You will be asked to compare some element of the two non-fiction sources. For example, you might have to write about the differences between characters or ideas. You will be expected to **summarise** those differences.

> **summarise**: give the main points more briefly in your own words

Timing

You will already have read the sources.

There are 8 marks for this question, which you will need to complete in 8 or 9 minutes.

What the examiner is looking for

The examiner is hoping you will have:
- shown a detailed understanding of whatever you have been asked to write about
- interpreted both explicit and implicit information in the sources
- linked evidence from the sources
- selected exactly the right quotations from both sources.

In this unit you will revise:
- identifying and summarising the required information
- presenting and comparing information from two texts.

Getting it right: Explicit information   REVISED

Read this extract, about Native Americans.

At the end of 1831 I was on the left bank of the Mississippi, at a place the Europeans call Memphis. While I was there, a numerous band of Choctaw Indians arrived; they were leaving their country and seeking to pass over to the right bank of the Mississippi, where they hoped to find an asylum promised to them by the American government. It was then the depths of winter, and that year the cold was exceptionally severe. The Indians brought their families with them; there were among them the wounded, the sick, newborn babies and old men on the point of death. They had neither wagons nor tents, but only some provisions and weapons. I saw them embark to cross the great river, and the sight will never fade from my memory. Neither sob nor complaint rose from that silent assembly. Their sufferings were of long standing, and they felt they could not be cured. All the Indians had already got into the boat that was to carry them across; their dogs were still on the bank. As soon as the animals finally realised that they were being left behind for ever, they all together raised a terrible howl and plunged into the icy waters of the Mississippi to swim after their masters.

Alexis de Tocqueville, *Democracy in America*, 1835

Tasks

1 What do we know about the Native Americans in this extract?

Focus on the explicit information, e.g.

They were leaving their country ...

They were crossing the Mississippi to find a safe place promised by the US government ...

You will not be listing details when you respond to Question 2. Instead, you will have to summarise the ideas.

When summarising, you need to:
- use your own words whenever possible (obviously, you will not change names and dates)
- only include what is relevant
- support what you say with quotations.

2 Summarise the details about the Indians, using your own words.

For example, you might begin:

The Native Americans were moving to another part of the country because the American government had said they could live there safely ...

Getting it right: Implicit information

REVISED

If you want to be successful in the exam, you need to be able to summarise what is implicit (what is suggested or inferred) as well as what is explicit.

To show understanding of what is inferred or suggested, you must interpret the details given: offer ideas that spring logically from what you have been told.

So, if someone were to say, 'I have just been to town and bought a new music system, a guitar and a whole wardrobe of new clothes', this could be suggesting that they are rich or have suddenly come into money.

Tasks

1 What is suggested about the plight of the Indians in each of the following phrases?
- ○ 'There were among them the wounded, the sick, newborn babies and old men on the point of death'
- ○ 'They had neither wagons nor tents'
- ○ 'Neither sob nor complaint arose from that silent assembly'
- ○ 'Their sufferings were of long standing, and they felt they could not be cured'
- ○ '(the dogs) raised a terrible howl and plunged into the icy waters of the Mississippi to swim after their masters'

2 Using the ideas you have collected, write a summary of what is inferred about the Indians in this extract.

You could begin:

The Indians seemed to be in a wretched state. They were travelling without tents or wagons, so we guess they might have been driven from their own land and not allowed to take anything with them ...

Getting it right: Blending explicit and implicit information

REVISED

You need to be able to blend explicit and implicit information into your answer and support what you say with quotations.

Tasks

1 Read this extract and decide what we know about the writer.

Write two lists:
○ what is explicit
○ what is implicit (suggested/inferred).

I discovered the other day that most of my underpants have been turned into dusters by the long-haired person who shares the house with me. I was a bit annoyed. I was quite attached to some of them. The paisley jockey shorts my Great Aunt Julia bought me for my 21st birthday and the boxer shorts with the slogan 'Over the Hill but not over the Hump' that my friends gave me one Christmas will be sorely missed. However, rather than start another war I left her polishing the coal scuttle with my memories and set off for the metropolis to buy some new pants. And it struck me as I wandered round goggling in the windows of shops how boring men's underwear is. I mean, without being sexist about it, most women's underwear is designed to be sexy – or at least to move things about a bit. Men's underwear seems to be there just to stop zips and seams causing rashes and watery eyes – in other words, it is purely functional. I think this is unfair – why can't men have sexy underwear too?

Mike Harding, *Hypnotising the Cat*, 1995

Summarising what we learn about the writer in this text, a Grade 5 student wrote:

inference →

support →

> The writer seems obsessed with underwear. ← overview
> We know that he is married, because he
> mentions 'the long haired person who shares ← quotation to support
> the house with me'. We know too that he
> doesn't want to argue with her. He then ← point unsupported
> thinks that women's underwear is more sexy
> than men's – he says 'it is designed to be
> sexy'. And he would like men's underwear
> to be sexy too ('why can't men have sexy
> underwear?').

Assessment comment

This response begins to interpret and chooses relevant quotations as evidence to support the points made. It is written in the student's own words.

To reach a higher standard, the response could have dealt with the writer's:
● humour
● attitude to women
● willingness to reveal his thoughts.

2 Write a summary of what we learn about the writer which includes the ideas above.

Getting it right: Presenting and comparing information from two texts

Comparison is a key element of this question.

Mark scheme

Grades	Descriptors
7, 8, 9	● Shows a detailed understanding of similarities/differences ● Interprets both sources in an intelligent way ● Blends evidence from the two sources effectively ● Selects a range of quotations from both sources, exactly the right ones to use
5, 6	● Clearly shows the similarities/differences between the two sources ● Begins to interpret both sources ● Shows clear connections between the sources ● Uses a range of relevant quotations from both sources
3, 4	● Writes about some similarities/differences ● Makes simple inference from one or both sources ● Tries to link points from the sources ● Uses quotations from both sources which might not always support the points
1, 2	● Recognises simple similarities/differences ● Writes about the sources without clarifying any inference ● Simple links or no links between the sources ● Simple references to details in the sources

It helps if you have a system for dealing with the two sources.

Consider this approach:
● Skim through the sources and underline or highlight relevant points to answer the question.
● Indicate which ones go together.

You can then:
● write about Source A
● deal with Source B, but mention the comparisons with Source A as they occur

or, to be more impressive,

● make regular comparisons between the sources throughout your answer, moving back and forth between them.

You will need words and phrases to make clear your links between the sources, for example:

'However …', 'In contrast …', 'On the other hand …', 'In Source B, though …', 'Whereas in Source A … in this case …', 'The differences are clear: in Source A … but in Source B …', 'Source A says … yet in Source B …'

> **Exam tip**
>
> The top band of marks asks for a blending of evidence from the two sources. Moving regularly between sources in your answer demonstrates that skill most effectively.

Read these extracts.

Source A: A newspaper report

A daring attempt at assassinating two members of the police was made on Wednesday night:- Between twelve and one o'clock, Constable Kenna was on duty when a man came up to him with a bundle under his arm. As he was passing, the constable stopped him and was interrogating him respecting the bundle, when the man suddenly produced a pistol and fired at the constable's breast, lodging the contents of the barrel in his chest. The constable fell on the ground. His murderous assailant made off, but he was encountered by Sergeant Kelly, who, having heard the shot, was hastening in that direction. The sergeant challenged the man, who instantly fired his revolver and shot the sergeant in the breast. Sergeant Kelly fell and the perpetrator of this double attempt at assassination made his escape, and has not yet been arrested. Some women who found the policemen lying bleeding and helpless gave the alarm, and a number of constables at once proceeded to the scene of this frightful outrage, and as quickly as possible conveyed the sufferers to Mercer's Hospital, where they received prompt attendance from the medical gentlemen. Having examined the men, Dr Butcher, the eminent surgeon, expressed his opinion that the wounds are likely to prove mortal.

Irish Catholic Chronicle And People's News of the Week, 1867

Source B: A newspaper article

The biggest modern crime mystery is this: where did the police disappear to? Not long ago, the patrolling constable in his distinctive helmet was a familiar sight in city and village. Now you can go for days without seeing anyone answering this description.

You might sometimes glimpse that completely different species, the modern copper. He – or she – is not a police officer as we used to know them, but a sort of paramilitary social worker, clattering with gadgets, tuned into a distant HQ through an earpiece, more distant, more nervous, more aggressive but strangely less powerful than he once was.

He is generally in a car swishing by too fast to see or hear anything. If on foot, he is seldom on regular patrol but hurrying to a meeting with a briefcase. Or he will be getting out of a big van with several others.

You would not want to catch his eye, even if you are doing nothing wrong. He is not friendly and patient like the old-time officers, but sternjawed and aloof.

He often has a shaved head and a slouching manner, not all that different from the bouncers lurking down the street outside the nightclub.

Sometimes he is actually armed. But even if he isn't carrying a gun, he looks as if he ought to be. Already on his crowded belt are handcuffs, a big club and a pepper spray. These items send the message that he is ready for anything, and not to be trifled with.

Peter Hitchens, *Mail Online*, 2014

Question: **What different impressions of the police are presented in these sources?**

Tasks

1 List points and supporting information from each source.
2 Draw lines between points which can be linked.
3 Read this Grade 6 response and take note of the annotations.

straightforward interpretation

relevant quotation

clear point, but unsupported

interpretation

inference

clear difference

another difference

> In Source A, the police are overcome by the man with the gun, who shot the constable then 'fired his revolver and shot the sergeant in the breast'. Both are unable to defend themselves and they will die ('the wounds are likely to prove mortal') – but other police come quickly to try to help them. In Source B, though, the writer just criticises the police for being 'sternjawed and aloof'. They are tough like 'bouncers' and seem 'paramilitary' so they seem to have little to fear. They have 'handcuffs, a big club and a pepper spray' and so might not be likely to end up 'bleeding and helpless' like the old fashioned policemen in Source A. Having said that, the writer does say a modern policeman is 'more aggressive but strangely less powerful than he once was' which seems strange when he is 'clattering with gadgets' but the old policemen cannot stop their assassination or catch the man who did it.

detail, supported

inference

Assessment comment

The answer becomes a little jumbled at the end, but does indicate differences and makes connections between them. It begins to interpret both sources and uses relevant quotations to support most of the points made.

4 How do the points made here compare with the ones you found?
5 How many more do you have which this response omitted?

Test yourself

TESTED

Write your response to the question, aiming to improve upon the answer above by:
- adding more comparisons
- including more detail.

How to prepare for the exam

It will be difficult to find nineteenth-century texts for practice purposes, but you can:
- read articles from newspapers and magazines and identify what they are saying and what they are suggesting
- find two modern articles on a similar subject and spot the differences in what they are saying – perhaps about a situation or about a person and what they have done.

Paper 2, Q3 Analysing persuasive language

What this question involves

You will be asked to analyse how language has been used in one of the non-fiction sources. The language is likely to have been used to give a viewpoint, to influence or to persuade.

Timing

You will already have read the source.

There are 12 marks for this question, which you will need to complete in 12 or 13 minutes.

What the examiner is looking for

The examiner is hoping you will have:
- analysed the words used
- quoted sensibly and appropriately
- used a range of subject terminology correctly.

In this unit you will revise:
- types of language
- how the audience is addressed
- how to analyse the language used.

In this case, look back at Paper 1, Question 2, because the language skills there are also applicable to Paper 2, Question 3.

> **Exam tip**
>
> You often use very similar skills in different parts of the exam: try not to see each question in isolation.

Types of language

When people are presenting ideas, they use a range of linguistic techniques.

Getting it right: Rhetorical and emotive language   REVISED

This is the speech made by Chief Joseph, leader of the Nez Perce tribe, when he was forced to surrender to the US army in 1877.

short, simple, moving sentences and phrasing throughout → I am tired of fighting. Our Chiefs are killed; Looking Glass is dead, Ta Hool Hool Shute is dead. The old men are all dead. It is the young men who say yes or no. He who led on the young men is dead. It is cold, and we have no blankets; the little children are freezing to death. My people, some of them, have run away to the hills, and have no blankets, no food. No one knows where are – perhaps freezing to death. I want to have time to look for my children, and see how many of them I can find. Maybe I shall find them among the dead. Hear me, my Chiefs! I am tired; my heart is sick and sad. From where the sun now stands, I will fight no more forever.

rhetorical: repetition and list of three

repetition: 'dead'

emotive detail

repetition and sense of despair

www.artofmanliness.com

rhetorical language: impressive language used to persuade, perhaps employing repetition, questions or dramatic detail

emotive language: language that affects the emotions

Task

1 Decide what you would say about how the **rhetorical** and **emotive language** is intended to affect the reader in the second half of the speech.

Getting it right: Facts and opinions

REVISED

This is an extract from an article about swearing:

> Britain is a nation of potty-mouthed potty trainers. A few years back, a survey of 3,000 11-year-olds revealed that nine out of ten parents swear in front of their children, and the average kid heard six different expletives per week (whoever said profanity was bad for your vocabulary?).
>
> Lauren Laverne, Observer Magazine, 2014

This is how a Grade 8 student wrote about the language:

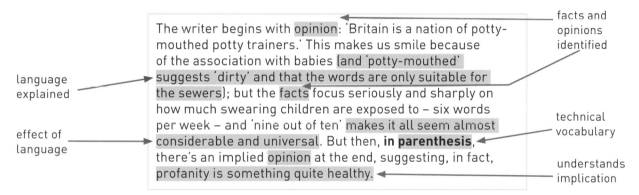

language explained

effect of language

facts and opinions identified

technical vocabulary

understands implication

The writer begins with opinion: 'Britain is a nation of potty-mouthed potty trainers.' This makes us smile because of the association with babies (and 'potty-mouthed' suggests 'dirty' and that the words are only suitable for the sewers); but the facts focus seriously and sharply on how much swearing children are exposed to – six words per week – and 'nine out of ten' makes it all seem almost considerable and universal. But then, **in parenthesis**, there's an implied opinion at the end, suggesting, in fact, profanity is something quite healthy.

Task

1 How are **facts** and **opinions** used to create interest in this report?

> Mysterious markings have been discovered at a National Trust property that archaeologists believe were intended to ward off evil spirits in the era of superstition and paranoia after the Gunpowder Plot to kill the king.
>
> 'Witchmarks' etched into floorboards at Knowle House in Kent are believed to have been made to protect the life of the superstitious King James I.
>
> They were discovered at Knowle by archaeologists investigating the Upper King's Room, which fell out of common use after the 17th century before being used for storage.
>
> Using tree ring dating, the conservationists from the Museum of London have dated the marks to early 1606 when King James was on the throne.
>
> Hannah Furness, 'Witchmarks, gunpowder plot and paranoia –
secrets under the floorboards', The Daily Telegraph, 2014

in parenthesis: an addition, in brackets or with commas, adding a personal detail or opinion

fact: something that can be proven

opinion: what someone thinks

Getting it right: Humour

Writers try to make us smile in a number of ways – for example, using:

- **sarcasm** ('If they call that helping the starving, I hope I'm never hungry')
- **irony** ('They told me to sit and wait my turn; every chair was taken.')
- exaggeration ('I spent eight hours looking for the right ward')
- a play on words ('We were more like poo relations than poor relations')
- contrasts ('To our left was the twinkling sea; to our right, the council tip') …

> **sarcasm**: a cutting remark, to make fun of somebody or someone
>
> **irony**: something which seems exactly the opposite of what might be expected, typically for a humorous effect

Here, a writer gives his views on a girl he liked in school:

> We would have an awkward conversation while she would flick her hair from one side to the other. This hair flicking was really quite something. She had fair hair in a bob and would move all of it to one side of her face and then a few moments later flick it back to the other side. It made me look like a tennis spectator, regularly shifting my head to the left and the right to follow it. It only added to the hypnotic effect she was having on me.
>
> We only had one 'date'. She said there wasn't the right chemistry between us. I was devastated, heartbroken, and blamed my chemistry teacher.
>
> Michael McIntyre, *Life and Laughing*, 2010

The writer:

- makes fun of himself (exaggerating with a simile: 'like a tennis spectator')
- uses **bathos** (moving from the list of devastation to a ridiculous idea: 'I was devastated, heartbroken, and blamed my chemistry teacher').

> **bathos**: anticlimax

Tasks

1 Write a short paragraph, explaining how the writer uses language to amuse the reader.

2 Explain how the writer uses language in this next extract, about Americans in Monument Valley, Utah. Try to comment on:
   - O the initial list
   - O the effect of 'disgorge'
   - O his sarcasm: 'They don't walk, they sort of roll …'
   - O the effect of the final simile.

> It's a funny thing but all the American programmes you see show healthy, neat, good-looking, slim and healthy people. Stand on the edge of Monument Valley watching the coaches disgorge the trippers and you'll get a very different picture. The Americans you see over there are often massively overweight and have spent so much time in their cars or as couch potatoes that they've forgotten what their legs are for. They don't walk, they sort of roll, like shell-suited amoeba.
>
> Mike Harding, *Hypnotising the Cat*, 1995

Getting it right: How the reader is addressed

Instead of adopting a humorous tone, the writer might use language in different ways – for example, language that sounds:

- angry ('This will never work! Things have to change.')
- critical ('Look carefully at what has happened: can anyone tell me it makes sense?')
- friendly ('I know, because I'm like you …').

The writer might use:

- first person ('I suspect that what I have experienced is quite normal …')
- second person ('You must make up your mind …')
- third person ('They have no choice. They have to be old men and old women.').

Tasks

1 How is language used for effect in the following extracts?
The first is done for you.

   a 'You are accepting things you should not; you are not chasing justice; you are allowing what is unfair to flourish and what is hurtful to grow.'

This is a Grade 9 response:

technical vocabulary

points supported throughout

understands the mood

writer's method

understands the message.

> The writer speaks directly to the reader, using a second person technique ('You … you …') and tries to make the message memorable by using a list of three, stressing the points with the repetition ('You are … you are …'), as if a table is being hammered. There is a tone of criticism throughout, with negativity stressed ('you should not' and 'not chasing'); and although 'flourish and 'grow' suggest life and development, they are linked to 'unfair' and 'hurtful', so it is the bad things that are increasing.

technique

effect

correct vocabulary

effect clarified

tone

understands the contrast

   b 'Because I have always loved this land – and I am not alone in this thought – I want to see it bloom and prosper. Together, our dreams can work miracles.'

   c 'Everyone should have a job that pays enough for them to live. No one should be forced to beg the state for help. We live in a rich country and that wealth should be for all, not for the few.'

2 In this extract, the writer is concerned with the behaviour of a child on an overnight flight. How does the language help get his reactions across to the reader? The annotations should help you answer.

How does this contrast with the passengers' mood?

Exaggeration?

> All of the passengers knew not only Jeffrey's name but also his age because, as he merrily ran about kicking their legs, he kept crying, 'I'm four years old!' I happened to have been spared his kicking my particular legs. Instead, he merely smeared chocolate on my shirt.
>
> And so, as our terror flight moved west, sleep was made impossible by the counterpoint of the voices of mother and son:
>
> 'Jeffrey, get down!'

What is the effect here?

Exam tip

Always remember to:
- use the correct vocabulary
- explain techniques and effects
- support with quotation.

'I'm four years old!'

'Jeffrey, now *look* what you've done to the man!'

Effect of speech? ———→ 'I'm four years old!'

If the passengers had been given a choice between riding with Jeffrey and riding with a hijacker, I know what their choice would have been. ◄——————— Tone?

Serious? What is the appeal to the reader throughout? ———→ As the plane moved west, the feelings of the passengers towards Jeffrey grew more intense. One gentleman invited him into the lavatory, to play with the blue water.

Bill Cosby, *Fatherhood*, 1986

Getting it right: Analysing the words used

REVISED ☐

You have to demonstrate the same kinds of skills here as for Paper 1, Question 2 (see pp. 14–19).

Mark scheme

Grade	Descriptors
7, 8, 9	● Analyses the effects of the words used ● Selects a range of quotations, exactly the right ones to use ● Uses all the correct subject terminology
5, 6	● Explains clearly the effects of the words used ● Uses a range of quotations that are relevant ● Uses subject terminology
3, 4	● Tries to comment on the words used ● Uses some relevant quotations ● Uses some subject terminology, but it is not always appropriate
1, 2	● Able to say simple things about the language ● Simple references to details in the source ● Some simple mention of subject terminology

The key element in the top bullet for each grade level is how well you deal with the language itself:
● For the lowest grades, you say simple things (e.g. 'The writer uses good adjectives').
● Better students comment (e.g. 'The adjectives suggest the sea is dangerous.').
● For Grades 5 or 6, comments are more detailed (e.g. 'The adjectives suggest the sea is dangerous, because …').
● The best students offer more interpretations (e.g. 'The adjectives imply that … and make the reader realise that … What is more, this effect contrasts with …').

This was written by a vicar who crossed the English Channel in 1835:

Wednesday – a day of mist, fog and despair. It blew a hurricane all that night, and we were kept awake by thinking of the different fish by which we should be devoured the following day. We were all up and at the quay by five in the morning. The captain hesitated over whether we should depart and your mother begged me not to do so. However, we embarked: the French Ambassador, ourselves, twenty Calais shopkeepers, and a variety of all nations. We, none of us, remember such a passage. I lay on the deck, shut my eyes and reflected that, as I have so little life to lose, it was of little consequence whether I drowned or died like a typical clergyman, from indigestion. Your mother arrived more dead than alive.

Nineteenth-century letters: A channel crossing

This is the beginning of a Grade 8 analysis of how the language creates a mood:

> The writer sets a miserable scene immediately – 'mist, fog and despair.' This tells us visibility was bad, but, just as importantly, gives us the mood ('despair'), as if they can see no hope because despair is the most awful emotion. The note setting the scene is a minor, incomplete sentence, the sort of jotting you might find in a diary – a personal reaction, the list of three revealing immediately the writer's state of mind.

Labels: mood, effect — analysis — technical term — style — understanding — technique

Task

1 Complete the analysis.

When you are writing about language try to offer detailed analysis rather than a rapid explanation of points.

Test yourself

TESTED ☐

This writer here is telling us about having to clear up the area around a school in Africa, after the holidays. It is full of trees and leaves.

How does he use language to gain the reader's sympathy?

Include:
- analysis of the language, technical terms and quotations
- mention of the writer's feelings and how he hopes to affect the reader.

'Get that all swept up!' the headmaster would tell us. 'I want the whole place cleaned up, at once!'

'At once!' There was enough work there, damned hard work, too, to last us for over a week. Especially since the only tools with which we were provided were our hands, our fingers, our nails.

'Now see it's done properly, and be quick about it,' the headmaster would say to the older pupils, 'or you'll have to answer for it!'

So at an order from the older boys, we would all line up like peasants about to reap or glean a field, and we would set to work like members of a chain-gang. In the schoolyard itself it wasn't too bad: the guava trees were fairly well spaced; but there was one part where the closely-planted trees grew in a hopeless tangle of leaves and branches. The sun could not penetrate here, and the acrid stench of decay lingered in the undergrowth even in the height of summer.

If the work was not going as quickly as the headmaster expected, the big boys, instead of giving us a helping hand, used to find it simpler to whip us with branches pulled from the trees. Now guava wood is regrettably flexible; skilfully handled, the springy switches used to whistle piercingly, and fall like flails of fire on our backsides. Our flesh stung and smarted, while tears of anguish sprang from our eyes and splashed on the rotting leaves at our feet.

Camara Laye, Dark Child, 1953

How to prepare for the exam

Read non-literary texts – like newspapers and magazine articles – and spot how the language is being used.

Underline significant words and phrases and annotate around them, saying what they suggest and how they affect the reader.

Paper 2, Q4 Comparing viewpoints and writers' methods

What this question involves

You will be asked to compare some element of the ideas and/or attitudes in the two non-fiction sources. For example, you might have to write about their different attitudes to war or to love. You will also have to analyse the **methods** they use to convey their message or feelings.

Timing

You will already have read the sources.

There are 16 marks for this question, which you will need to complete in 16 or 17 minutes.

What the examiner is looking for

The examiner is hoping you will have:
- shown a detailed and perceptive understanding of the differences between the two writers' ideas and attitudes
- analysed and compared the methods
- selected exactly the right quotations from both sources.

In this unit you will revise:

how to write about and compare:
- writers' ideas and attitudes
- writers' methods.

> **methods**: these might be the approaches used (humour/being coldly critical/basing the text on facts or anecdotes/using comparison/moving through stages to a 'big finish' ...); but you might also include how language is used differently in the texts.

Getting it right: Writers' attitudes   REVISED

To decide on a writer's attitude does not mean to simply know what he or she says: you need to identify their point of view and, beyond that, their precise ideas.

Consider this extract, written this century.

> When I was a boy I grew up on a council estate in Newport that was 99% white. When I went out, I did not walk around the estate, I had to fight my way around. Every day I would be targeted, often with actual violence, more often with verbal insults. Imagine having to put up with that, not because of what you've said or what you've done, but all because of the colour of your skin.
>
> I have spent my adult life working to make sure that can never happen again, hoping that all that is finally in the dark and distant past. I'm really hopeful of change and there has been a shift in attitudes right across society, but one institution seems immune to that change – and that is football.
>
> Nathan Blake, *Wales Online*, 2014

The text is about racism, but what, *exactly*, is the writer saying?

Tasks

1 Complete this list of the points made:
   - Because he was in a minority, his life was a battle
   - …

2 Sum up his attitude in just one sentence.

Your summative sentence might say something like:

> The writer has suffered from bullying in his own life and has worked to improve the situation – he now feels it is improving, but not in the world of football.

To respond in the exam, you might choose to offer a summing up of the writer's views, then work through the precise ideas and details.

3 Use that approach to answer this question:

What is the writer saying about racism?

Next, consider this text, from an American politician writing about slavery in 1863.

> Slavery must be resisted, not only on political grounds, but on all other grounds, whether social, economic, or moral. Ours is a solemn battle between Right and Wrong; between Good and Evil. Such a battle cannot be fought with excuses.
>
> Senator Davis from Mississippi claims 'Slavery is but a form of civil government for those who are not fit to govern themselves'; and his colleague, Mr Brown, says it 'is a great moral, social and political blessing – a blessing to the slave and a blessing to the master.' One senator from Virginia claims it is 'best for the happiness of both races'.
>
> Yet, I oppose the essential Barbarism of Slavery, in all its influences. Slavery must be exposed in its truly hateful character.

Charles Sumner, Barbarism of Slavery, 1860

This is a Grade 5 standard explanation of the writer's attitude:

sums up the writer's viewpoint ——
lacking detail
analyses the term of insult ——
explanation ——

> The writer opposes slavery. He believes it is 'Wrong' and 'Evil' and that there can be no excuses that make it seem acceptable. He points out that some men try to defend it, and gives their views on why it is a good thing. He, though, calls it 'Barbarism', which makes it sound primitive and uncivilised. He says it is 'hateful', which must be how he feels about it himself.

selects supporting quotations
—— his belief
—— the opposite viewpoint

A better response might have added:
- mention of the importance of 'slavery must be resisted …'
- an explanation of the point about 'social, economic or moral' evil
- a section on exactly how he seems to feel about the precise arguments of slavery's supporters (because of the precise words he has chosen to quote e.g. 'blessing', compared to 'Barbarism')
- an explanation of the phrase 'Slavery must be exposed'.

Exam tip

There is not time to include all the points made in a lengthy exam source: in the exam, identify the main ideas and deal with those in detail.

Getting it right: Comparing ideas and attitudes

Of course, in the examination you have to compare the two sources.

Look back to pages 41–43 and remind yourself of how to compare.

In the case of the two texts you have just been examining, you might:
- begin with their two standpoints (e.g. one has suffered from racism, but believes the situation is improving though there is still much to be done in the world of football; the other is preaching about the evil that is slavery, saying it is wrong and revealing some of the unacceptable things people say about it)
- then work through precisely what they believe, making comparisons as you go (e.g. 'I'm really hopeful of change'/'Slavery must be opposed').

Task

1 Write a comparison of the writers' attitudes to racial inequality.

Consider these two texts.

Text A: A letter from a Scottish farmer, written from Argentina in 1891

I write you a few lines to let you know that I went over to Patagonia to try and start sheep farming. We arrived in Punta Arenas all right after a very rough passage, then rode up through Patagonia for about three hundred miles to Port San Julian & bought 1200 sheep there and we are just busy shearing them. We are sending the wool home to England. There is a ship coming and taking out stores for us and taking away the wool. Do not be surprised at me being so long in writing for I am not very near a post office. It is about 300 miles to the nearest and it is seldom there is a chance to send letters away. There is a fellow starting away from here tomorrow to go down south so I am taking the chance to send them with him. It is rather a rough life over here. We have got no houses, only a sort of mud cabin to live in, but we get along not so bad. I have not even a table to lay the paper on to write the letter. I am sitting holding it on my knee and writing it but I hope there may be better days in store for us before long. If once I get a piece of camp secure, I think I will soon get along, at least I hope so. Only there is a beast they call the lion here that is very bad on the sheep. It is a species of the cat tribe. It can kill a sheep with one stroke of the paw. Sometimes one or two will come in the night among the sheep and do great damage.

George Anderson, 1891

Text B: From a recent travel guide to Port San Julian

The quiet port town of San Julián, has a fascinating history, although little of it is in evidence today. The first Mass in Argentina was held here in 1520 after the Portuguese explorer Magellan had executed a member of his mutinous crew. Then in 1578, Francis Drake also put in here to behead Thomas Doughty, after amiably dining with him. There's plenty of wildlife to be seen in the area, and a paradise of marine life in the coastal Reserva Natural San Julián, all very accessible from the town.

The current town was founded in 1901 on a peninsula overlooking a fine natural harbour, as a port to serve the sheep farmers of this part of Santa Cruz. It's a lovely location and the concentration of marine life is stunning. The best time to visit is in December to see dolphins and cormorants, though there's plenty to see from December to April. Cabo Curiosa, 15 km north, has fine beaches: there are 30 km of spectacular coastline, and it's a popular bathing place for the whole of the region. You can also visit the ruins of Florida Blanca, 10 km west, the site of the failed colony founded in 1870 by Antonio Viedma. It's certainly worth visiting Estancia La María, 150 km west, one of the main archaeological sites in Patagonia: a huge canyon with 87 caves of paintings including human hands 4000–12,000 years old.

www.footprinttravelguides.com

Tasks

1 Complete this table, to compare the writers' attitudes to Port San Julian.

	Text A	Text B
Overall attitude	Life there is difficult and primitive. It seems a long way from civilisation.	
Details that support their views (to compare, where possible)	'It is rather a rough life over here'	'It's a lovely location'

> **Exam tip**
>
> You have sufficient time in the exam to quickly produce a similar table. Alternatively, you can highlight the important details and, perhaps, draw lines between those that you intend to compare.

2 Write a response which compares their different attitudes.

Getting it right: Comparing writers' methods

REVISED ☐

To write about methods, you might want to analyse:
- the writer's viewpoint (e.g. first person or third person)
- the writer's attitude (e.g. angry, subtle …)
- how the reader is addressed (e.g. as someone who can help or someone who needs to be convinced)
- approaches (e.g. humour, repetition, anecdote, the use of quotations, rhetorical questions or statistics, imagery, listing, emotive language …)
- particular words used (e.g. depressing adjectives, stirring verbs, semantic fields relating to love or hate …)
- imagery (e.g. similes, metaphors…)
- the use of sentences (e.g. to create excitement, climax, contrast …)

Re-read the extracts about Port San Julian. You are now going to compare the methods the writers use to get across their feelings about the place.

Tasks

1 Read these exemplar extracts from student responses and notice how much more detailed the second one is; and how it focuses more on effects.

This is how a Grade 3 student began:

method and effect

details indicating how the letter is written

> They both write about San Julian but in different ways. Text A sounds as if he's not having a good time. He's writing a letter, so he's writing to people he knows, so he tells them things that aren't very nice. He sounds quite fed up to get their sympathy. He tells them what is happening to the sheep and about the beast to try to get their sympathy. Text B just says lots of things about why the place is good.

method

contrasting method, but lacks detail at this point

This was written by a Grade 9 student:

audience – which affects a writer's approach

comparison

method

effect

well-selected supports

> The farmer writes a letter, presumably to friends or family, so he relays honest details about the hardships in San Julian. In contrast, the travel guide presents welcoming facts to the world, to lure potential visitors to the port. It begins: 'The quiet port town ...' which makes it seem like a restful world away from it all, whereas the letter begins with mention of 'a very rough sea passage' and a three-hundred mile ride – facts designed to create the impression he is living in a difficult place, far from civilisation.

method

effect

comparison

effect

2 Complete this table, to clarify exactly what other methods the farmer is using to clarify his attitude in Text A.

Method	Supporting detail/effect
some narrative	
sense of isolation	
the basic nature of their life	
wildness emphasised by the 'beast'	
details of basic housing	
hope for a better future, rather than being totally convinced	
repetition of 'rough'	
first person, speaking directly to a second	
all one paragraph	

3 Draw up a similar table to clarify what methods are used in Text B.
4 Use the two tables to write a comparison of the methods used by the two texts.

You might decide to compare:

- their appeal to different audiences
- how the reader is addressed
- the focus on history and attractions as opposed to the focus on the farmer's life
- the different sorts of details included
- the use of facts
- the kinds of language used.

Getting it right: Analysing methods

You have already dealt with analysing language (see Paper 1, Question 2 and Paper 2, Question 3); producing an analysis of methods should follow the same pattern:

- identify the method
- quote appropriately
- try to offer a range of ideas.

This is from a newspaper description of Whitechapel in London in 1888, when Jack the Ripper was on the loose and murdering women:

> The street is oppressively dark, though at present the gloom is relieved somewhat by feebly lighted shopfronts. Men are lounging at the doors of the shops, smoking evil-smelling pipes. Women with bare heads and with arms under their aprons are sauntering about in twos and threes, or are seated gossiping on steps leading into pitch dark passages. Now round the corner into another still gloomier passage, for there are no shops here to speak of. This is the notorious Wentworth Street. The police used to make a point of going through this only in couples, and possibly may do so still when they go there at all. Just now there are none met with.

Daily News, November 1888

Here is part of a Grade 8 analysis of how the writer presents the area:

writer's technique — The writer uses concentrated detail and begins by establishing a grim setting. The first sentence opens with 'oppressively dark': light is 'feeble', pipes are 'evil-smelling', passages are 'pitch dark' or 'gloomier'. The semantic field suggests an atmosphere of evil and danger is everywhere, and the place is unhappy, dismal. Then people are introduced – and they fit the scene. The women there are presented as poor ('bare heads, 'aprons') but the writer implies they get no protection, because there are no police.

method
draws together relevant language
analysis
another method
implication
analysis

Tasks

1 Decide what more you might say about some of the language, e.g.
- 'oppressively dark'
- 'sauntering'.

2 What is the effect of the final sentence?

In 1906, another writer thinks the Ripper might have used the Tube.

> Perhaps he travelled to Whitechapel by the underground railway, often late at night. Probably on several occasions he had but one fellow passenger in the compartment with him, and that might have been a woman. Imagine what the feelings of those travellers would have been had they known that they were alone in the dark tunnels of the Underground with Jack the Ripper?'

> George Sims, *The Mysteries of Modern London*, 1906

The method here is to present the situation and have the reader think about the implications.

Task

1 Analyse the methods used to frighten the reader. Think about:
   ○ the way we focus on a scene, rather than just an idea
   ○ how suggestions are made ('Perhaps', 'Probably', 'Imagine')
   ○ how terror is suggested in the last sentence
   ○ the use of the rhetorical question.

Getting it right: Comparing writers' attitudes and analysing methods

REVISED

In the exam, you will have to compare the writers' attitudes and ideas as well as analysing their methods, all in one single answer.

This means blending the skills you have been revising in this unit.

Read these two texts, about wild creatures.

Text A: An account by a woman scientist of how she was attacked by a huge bear in the wilderness in Canada

The bear had no intention of leaving me alone. After chewing on my right shoulder, arm and side repeatedly, the bear began to bite my head and tear at my scalp. As I heard the crunching sound of the bear's teeth biting into my skull, I realised it was all too hopeless. I remember thinking, 'This has got to be the worst way to go.' I knew it would be a slow death. My fate was to bleed to death.

All of a sudden, the bear clamped its jaws into me and began dragging me by the right arm down the slope through the brush, over rocks and through brush. Then it walked about four feet away and sat down to rest.

Here, I thought, might be a chance to save myself – if only I could get at my walkie-talkie. Slowly I moved my left arm, which was still undamaged, behind me and into my pack. I pulled out my radio, turned it on, pulled up two or three segments of the antenna, and pushed in the button. Holding it close to my mouth, I said as loudly as I dared, 'Ed, this is Cynthia. Come quick, I'm being eaten by a bear.'

Cynthia Dusel-Bacon, in *Bear Attacks, their causes and avoidance*, 1985

Text B: A newspaper report from 1886 about a wild man in Ohio

A party of hunters, who have just returned from the hills of Holmes County, Ohio, say they encountered a curious creature on their trip. According to their description, a wild man, or some other strange being, is at large. The hunters were surprised to see what they describe as a man, entirely nude, but covered with what appeared to be matted hair. When seen he was some distance away, but he started towards them on a run, and gave forth strange guttural sounds. The party of hunters, which included four persons, all armed with guns, broke and ran. The strange creature turned back and was seen to enter Killbuck Creek. On approaching the water, he dropped on all fours and plunged in like a dog, swimming in the manner similar to a canine. The hunters did not have the nerve to return, but got away from the place as soon as possible.

The Indiana Weekly Progress, 1886

Tasks

1 Write lists of:
   o Text A's ideas about the bear and attitudes to it
   o the methods the writer of Text A has used to capture the experience and create an impression of the creature
   o Text B's ideas and about the wild man and attitudes to him
   o the methods the writer of Text B has used to capture the experience and create an impression of the creature.

To compare these two texts, you might:
● compare the ideas and attitudes and then compare the methods; or
● offer a comparison which blends the different elements.

Either approach is acceptable.

Don't worry if you decide to write about ideas and attitudes first but then find yourself including points which are really about methods (language analysis, for example). You will still be credited for the ideas.

> **Exam tip**
>
> Try out both approaches and see which works best for you. It is worth investing the time, because it is likely to make your exam performance better.

Consider this extract from the opening of a response which is blending the ideas and methods:

well-selected quotations throughout → / different interpretations: analysis / range of attitudes / comparison begins / perspective / comparison →

method / effect / implies attitude to bear / attitude / analysis of attitude / comparisons / understands method

Text A is a first-person narrative which has the detail to show us exactly how the writer is suffering. The verbs 'chewing', 'bite' and 'tear' show the violence of the attack and suggest what the effect must have been on the writer – intense pain, obviously. Having said that, she continues like the scientist she is – amazingly calm, objective and accepting: 'My fate was to bleed to death'. There is no sense of hatred towards the bear. She seems to see it as a wild creature which, perhaps, knows no better and almost sounds like a pet ('It walked about four feet away and sat down to rest.') The attitude in Text B is very different. This is a newspaper report and is not so emotive. Like Text A, it tells a story, but creates the impression of someone speaking in a courtroom ('According to their description ...'). In a totally different way to Text A, it is all still very serious ...

2 Obviously, the extract above is only a beginning, but read the mark scheme on page 60 and decide which band of marks the response might fall into. Consider each descriptor carefully, and decide what more the student would need to do to reach a Grade 9.

Mark scheme

Grade	Descriptors
7, 8, 9	• Able to write in detail about the differences in the writers' ideas and attitudes • Compares the ideas and attitudes intelligently • Analyses the effects of the methods used by the writers • Selects a range of quotations, exactly the right ones to use
5, 6	• Shows clearly how the ideas and attitudes are different • Compares the ideas and attitudes clearly • Explains clearly how methods have been used by the writers • Uses a range of quotations that are relevant
3, 4	• Able to write about some differences between the ideas and attitudes • Tries to compare the ideas and attitudes • Tries to comment on the words used • Uses some quotations (possibly from just one source)
1, 2	• Simple references to the differences in ideas and attitudes • Able to indicate different ideas and attitudes • Can say simple things about how the writers have presented the ideas and perspectives • Simple references to details in one or both sources

Typical mistakes

• Writing about the sources without making comparisons
• Focusing on just the ideas or just the methods without dealing with the other element

Test yourself

TESTED ☐

Reread the two texts about the bear and the wild man, then, using the lists you made, write a full answer of your own to this task:

Refer to **both** Text A and Text B.

Compare how the two writers convey their different attitudes to the wild creatures.

In your answer, you should:
- compare their different attitudes
- compare the methods they use to convey their attitudes
- support your ideas with quotations from both texts.

How to prepare for the exam

Don't worry about the fact that in the exam one of the texts will be from the nineteenth century. For extra practice, simply find two articles about the same subject – whatever is in the news – and try to decide on the writers' viewpoints and the methods they have used to get their message across. How are they different?

If you invest in a copy of *The Daily Mirror* and *The Daily Telegraph* on the same day, there should be enough material to keep you going for a while!

You can also practise without comparison by examining any article on its own.

What does Section B involve?

What you have to do ...

On both papers, you should have spent approximately 60 minutes on Section A, which leaves you 45 minutes for Section B. You will have to produce just one response for Section B on both papers.

What you will have to write

Paper 1

Paper 1 will give you a choice of questions and you must choose just one of them. You will be presented with:

- two questions asking you to describe; or
- two questions asking you to produce a piece of narrative writing (story); or
- one question asking you to produce a piece of description and one asking you to write a narrative.

It is unwise to try to answer both questions, because then both the responses tend to be rushed and often underdeveloped and although your best mark will count towards your total, the mark for both is likely to be disappointing. Instead, decide which question you can handle best and try to respond carefully and in detail.

Paper 2

You will have no choice on Paper 2.

You will have to answer the one question offered, which will ask for your point of view on some issue. You will be told the topic, the audience you are writing for (for example, the Prime Minister, or readers of a national newspaper) and the form of writing you have to produce (perhaps a speech or an article or a letter).

How to divide up your time

If you are wise, you will spend:

- four or five minutes planning
- 35 minutes writing
- five minutes checking and improving your work.

It is worth remembering that the best responses are almost always planned in advance and checked carefully at the end; the most disappointing are jumbled and full of basic errors that could have been corrected easily.

> **Exam tip**
>
> There are no marks for neatness. Altering and improving your writing will improve your grade, not harm it.

The marks will be awarded in the same way for both papers.

24 marks	For content and organisation	Ideas, ability to target purpose and audience, structure, paragraphing and use of language
16 marks	For technical accuracy	Sentences, punctuation, spelling, vocabulary and use of Standard English

Importantly, do not think that the more you write, the higher your mark will be. Examiners are looking for quality, not quantity. It is far better to produce two and a half pages of interesting and accurate writing than to write five pages that are unstructured and full of repetition and errors.

Communicating effectively: tone, style and register

What this skill involves

You need to know about three different forms of writing: description and narrative (Paper 1) and writing with a point of view (Paper 2). You must write for the specified purpose; and when offering a viewpoint you will also have to write in a given form (article, letter, speech …) for a particular audience (newspaper readers, school governors …)

Timing

You have 45 minutes to complete your response. There are 40 marks for each Section B question, 24 of which are for content and organisation. That mark includes how well you have targeted the necessary purpose, form and audience.

What the examiner is looking for

The examiner is hoping you will have:
- written in an appropriate way about the topic or title you have been given (purpose)
- produced a response which reads like a letter, article or whatever is required (form)
- written appropriately for the reader (audience).

In this unit you will revise:

how to impress the examiner. You will focus on how to:
- identify the purpose, form and audience
- write appropriately for them.

Getting it right: Identifying the purpose, form and audience

The tasks on Paper 1 are very predictable: you will be writing a description or a narrative and you must assume the response is for the examiner. For example:

form →

purpose → **Write the opening of a novel entitled 'The World's End'.**

On Paper 2, you need to be aware of form as well. For example:

form →

audience →

Write a letter to your local council to express your views on their proposal to build a new housing estate close to where you live. ← purpose

Tasks

1 Identify the purpose, form and audience in each of these tasks:
   ○ Write a description of the best place you have ever visited.
   ○ Write a short story which begins 'There seemed to be no hope.'
   ○ A recent television programme claimed 'The way we are going, the world will not survive into the next century.'
2 Write a letter to a broadsheet newspaper, giving your views on this idea.

Getting it right: Producing what is required

Purpose: Make sure you do exactly what the title specifies. So, if, for example, you are instructed to 'describe an unusual journey', you should not write about what happened when you were on holiday: the journey is what matters.

Form: You will lose marks if you are instructed to write a letter but produce an article.

Audience: Especially when giving a viewpoint, try to show awareness of your audience. So, you might want to flatter ('You are well-respected ...'), appeal to their intelligence ('Naturally, someone with your education will be aware that ...'), or amuse ('Ironically, I was the one caught with my trousers down ...').

> **Typical mistakes**
> - Misreading the question
> - Not planning, so that the intended focus is lost
> - Not targeting an educated audience

Tasks

1 A student was given this task: **Write a page for your school's website, giving your views on why yours is a good school.**

What is wrong with his opening?

> OK, we all know that there are a lot of schools around, right? But I think that ours is ace and that's why everyone should come here. It's got lots of things going for it and ace teachers and stuff. I'm like, 'Wow come on and enjoy it with us, man.'

> **Exam tip**
>
> Examiners look for excellence. You should always:
> - write in the best, formal Standard English you know – unless you are using dialogue or quoting someone
> - aim to impress with your paragraphs, sentences, punctuation and vocabulary.

Clearly, there are problems with:
- Standard English
- vocabulary
- repetition
- understanding of the audience.

2 Write a more appropriate opening.

Mark scheme

Bear in mind this mark scheme for purpose, form and audience:

Grades	Descriptors
7, 8, 9	Perfectly matched to purpose, form and audience
5, 6	Clearly targeting purpose, form and audience
3, 4	Attempts to target purpose, form and audience
1, 2	Simple awareness of purpose, form and audience

Test yourself

1 Identify, as appropriate, the purpose, form and audience in each of the following:
- Describe an old house.
- Write a short story in which an accident plays an important part.
- Write the text of a speech you are going to give to a conference of local employers, giving your views on why work experience is important to young people in school.

2 Write a brief but appropriate opening to each task.

How to prepare for the exam

Choose some of the Section B essay titles in this section of this book (see p. 62–102). Identify the purpose, form and audience in each case. Write openings which you feel would impress by being appropriate in terms of purpose, form and audience.

Organising your writing

What this skill involves

On both papers, you will have 45 minutes to produce a written response for Section B. However, your writing needs to be planned before you start because a clear structure is needed if you are to communicate effectively with the reader.

You need to get your ideas into a suitable order, so that they flow logically and convincingly to your ending.

Timing

You can only allow about four or five minutes to complete your plan. You will then have about 35 minutes to write your response and five minutes left to check through it and improve it at the end.

What the examiner is looking for

The examiner is hoping to read a response which:
● develops logically
● avoids repetition
● includes high-quality features (such as imagery, quotation, examples …) and a range of vocabulary and punctuation
● moves from an engaging opening to a memorable ending.

In this unit you will revise:

how to organise your writing. You will focus on how to:
● plan
● produce effective openings and endings.

Exam tip

If you have a plan, you won't forget to write in paragraphs; you won't forget to include important things; and it will help you finish on time, because you know exactly how much more you have to write.

Getting it right: Planning   REVISED

If you have a planning system, you can use it for both papers – and for other subjects too. This four-stage system is simple and proven.

A planning system

1 Underline the important words in the title.
2 Make a spider diagram of ideas.
3 Turn those ideas into a list, so that you know the order in which you will deal with them. Leave three or four lines beneath each sub-heading.
4 Fill in the lines you have left with details of what you will put in that section or paragraph.

Consider this Paper 2 task:

the form – suggests the style you should adopt

always required for Paper 2

① **Write a newspaper article to give your views on whether more foreign languages should be taught in schools.**

the focus

② <u>Spider diagram</u>

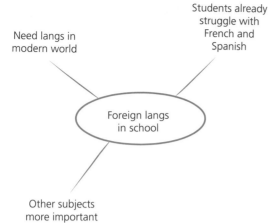

Tasks

1 Add two or three more ideas you could write paragraphs about.

③ <u>Listing</u>

Having turned the ideas into a list, a student has filled in some of the gaps, to indicate what each section or paragraph will include.

<u>Section 1: Intro</u> –

'Have people who dream up these ideas ever been into a real school?'

anecdote of Salim, who already has to deal with five different languages – be emotive

use semi-colons to list his pressures

'Can the average student cope with any more?'

<u>Section 2: Problems with French and Spanish at present</u> –

shortage of high-quality lang teachers – 30% of trainees leaving teaching within 3 yrs

Attempt to introduce Mandarin at this academy failed (teachers didn't know enough/ students refused to co-operate – use colon)

Use sarcasm – which langs do govt ministers speak?

So many students have only basic English – focus on that!

<u>Section 3: Congested timetable.</u>

Other things need to be remedied first.

No time for sport at present

Two English subjects in just 3 hrs a week – crazy

Almost everyone in the world speaks English, so Maths and Science more vital here

<u>Section 4 ...</u>

<u>Section 5 ...</u>

<u>Section 6: Conclusion</u> –

---

2 Complete this detailed plan with ideas of your own.
3 Complete the full planning process for this Paper 1 task:
Write a short story set on a holiday beach.

Exam tip

Put as many ideas as you can into your plan. It saves time when you are writing because you won't lose vital minutes having to stop and think.

This is the mark scheme for the basic organisation of ideas:

Grades	Descriptors
7, 8, 9	● Highly organised, and incorporating many complex ideas ● Consistently well-organised paragraphs, linked fluently with integrated connectives
5, 6	● Interesting writing, with detailed and connected ideas ● Suitable paragraphs throughout, with connectives to link ideas
3, 4	● A variety of linked and relevant ideas ● Some paragraphs and connectives
1, 2	● A few ideas, possibly linked ● Random attempts at paragraphs, or no paragraphs at all

Tasks

1 Try to decide where your plan might fit into this mark scheme.
(You will be unable to assess the quality of connectives at this stage.)

2 Look again at each of your paragraphs. Could you organise the ideas into a better order within each paragraph? You can always number the points, to indicate the order in which you will deal with them.

Getting it right: Openings and endings

REVISED

Obviously, the whole of your response is important, but you should focus especially on:

● the opening, because the examiner immediately gets an impression of you and the likely quality of your writing

● the ending, because it is the last thing the examiner reads before putting a mark on your work.

Here are two openings in which the students are giving their views on the importance of work experience.

Student A:

I hated work experience in Boots. I had to work from nine in the morning til five in the afternoon. My supervisor was called Mavis. I had to stack shelves and clean up and make tea for everybody. It was dead boring.

Student B:

I have to admit that the whole idea of work experience terrified me. I was sent out to spend two weeks in a local garage, and I'd heard tales of students from our school being sent there before, and they'd had their trousers ripped off and oil smeared all over their …   That's what I'd heard anyway, and regularly. It was a very worrying prospect. I was not looking forward to my time at Gary's Auto-Repair Shop one little bit.

Tasks

1 Which is from a Grade 3 response and which is from a Grade 7 response? Why is the better one so much more interesting?

The second response ended like this:

So suddenly, it was all over and I had loved it and would recommend it to everybody. I had no fears left, good friends I was sorry to leave; and there hadn't been a spot of oil inside my jeans. Why was I so worried in the first place? They have even offered me a Saturday job, so it must have gone well. Of course, if I hear that anyone else is being dispatched there for work experience, I'll definitely give them the best advice: 'Be careful, buddy – engine oil is difficult to get out of your underwear.'

After all, overcoming the fear is a large part of the pleasure, when you look back.

Test Yourself answers at **www.hoddereducation.co.uk/myrevisionnotes/gcse-english-language**

2 What is good about the ending?

You should have spotted the student used:
- connectives: 'so', 'of course' and 'after all'
- a quotation
- a rhetorical question
- humour
- semi-colons, speech marks, a question mark and commas
- a short paragraph for the 'big finish'.

Importantly, too, the ending links back to the start. It is still focused because it's about the experience at the garage and the initial fear being unnecessary; but there is also the reference back to the oil down the jeans, demonstrating that the response had been carefully planned.

Exam tip

Your response will always seem more impressive if your ending links back to your opening.

Tasks

1 What is disappointing about this opening sentence?

> In this essay I am going to give my point of view on the subject of punishment in schools.

2 Why would this ending fail to impress?

> So I have given my views on what is wrong with punishments in school and I have told you why some people think punishments are all right and why some people think they should be different.

3 How might they both be improved?

It is always advisable to try to avoid:
- repeating the question
- stating the obvious, unless it is for a particular purpose.

4 Write a better opening and an ending of your own on this topic. You might decide to:
- begin with a question or an example
- use a list of three, a simile, emotive language or sarcasm or any feature that makes the reader more interested.

Typical mistakes

Especially when they are in an examination situation, students:
- don't bother to plan
- plan, but then don't follow the plan
- fail to include features that will impress the examiner
- don't keep their eye on the clock
- fail to check through and correct what they have written.

Test yourself

 TESTED ☐

Plan – in detail – and then write the opening and ending for this task:
Describe the most interesting place you have ever been.
Try to:
- complete your plan as quickly as possible – in 4 or 5 minutes if you can
- put interesting features into your opening and ending, to impress the examiner
- ensure there is a link between your start and finish.

How to prepare for the exam

Set your own essay titles and practise planning them. They can be on any subject: why not set yourself a title on your favourite sport or pastime? Then on your family ... Each time you complete a plan, you will be becoming more efficient at the planning prcess.

Obviously, you could then write the full response, but perhaps you could focus just on the opening and ending. Aim to make them good enough to impress the examiner.

Exam tip

Planning becomes quicker with practice. The time you spend practising is an investment. Don't think that you need not bother and that you will just be able to produce a detailed plan on the day of the exam, because that is most unlikely.

Even Olympic medallists have to train!

Using effective punctuation

What this skill involves

You will be assessed in part on how well you punctuate in Section B. You will be rewarded for using a range of punctuation accurately and effectively.

What the examiner is looking for

The examiner is hoping you will have:
- used a wide range of punctuation – moving beyond just full-stops and capital letters
- punctuated in the right places, using the correct punctuation marks
- used your punctuation imaginatively.

In this unit you will revise:

how to use:
- capital letters, full stops, commas, question marks and exclamation marks
- speech marks
- apostrophes, colons and semi-colons
- brackets, dashes and ellipses
- punctuation impressively.

Getting it right: Capitals, full stops, commas, question marks and exclamation marks

REVISED

Notice how the punctuation has been used here:

> The door was white, with a small window in the middle. Had it always been so pretty? Probably not, Maisie thought. Or maybe when she was younger she did not even notice!

You will be expected to use:
- capitals to start sentences and for names
- full stops at the ends of sentences
- commas to indicate additions to sentences: e.g. **subordinate clauses**
- question marks and exclamation marks appropriately.

> **Exam tip**
>
> Take care with exclamation marks. Try not to use more than one or two – to indicate emotion – in any response.

> **subordinate clause**: a clause that makes no sense without a main clause

Getting it right: Speech marks

REVISED

You are likely to use speech in description or narrative; and you might use quotation in your viewpoint response.

Notice the rules here:

> 'He chews hammers,' said Rani.
>
> 'He does what?' asked Sajida.
>
> Rani repeated, 'He chews hammers!'
>
> 'Gosh. Does he do it for a living?' said Rani. 'I mean, is he a professional?'
>
> 'No. He isn't. I just told you,' said Rani, 'that he's an 'ammer chewer.'

Test Yourself answers at **www.hoddereducation.co.uk/myrevisionnotes/gcse-english-language**

The rules

- One speaker per paragraph.
- Speech marks around the words actually spoken.
- Always punctuate before closing speech marks.
- 'he said/she replied' etc. following speech have lower case.
- When speech is interrupted in the middle by the person speaking:
  - ○ if 'he said' or something similar breaks two complete sentences, put a full stop and begin the speech with a capital
  - ○ if it comes in the middle of a sentence, put a comma and then the person carries on speaking with a lower case letter.

Task

1 Write a short conversation, using the rules above.

Getting it right: Apostrophes, colons and semi-colons

REVISED

There are two uses for **apostrophes**:
- when something is omitted
- when something belongs to someone or something.

one person owns the hat → 'That's Steve's hat.'

omission →

'I don't believe you. He shares it with Will. It's the boys' hat.' ← more than one person owns

'They should donate it to the nation. It could be the people's hat.' ← owned by a plural noun

Task

1 Correct the following:

> Jay borrowed Jeds jumper and both his cousins best shirts. Didnt he look stupid when they wouldnt fit in his bag!

A **colon** follows a general statement and introduces a list. So, we might have:
- Sue loved ice cream, chocolate and cola.
  but
- Sue loved most of the things that were bad for her: ice cream, chocolate and cola.

A **semi-colon** breaks up a complicated list:
- Sue loved most things that were bad for her: ice cream, which came in huge pots that she emptied within a day; chocolate, that she bought each day on the way to college; and cola, which she drank with every meal.

or separates two closely-related sentences:
- The time to act is now; tomorrow might be too late.

Task

1 Write a short description of your favourite meal. Include:
  - ○ a colon
  - ○ semi-colons, used in different ways.

Getting it right: Brackets, dashes and ellipses

These elements of punctuation add variety.

Dyta (whose mother was a hairdresser) loved me – goodness knows why – and wanted to get married ...

— adds information
— used to add an informal thought
— suggests there is more to come

Task

1 Add another section to your meal description, including brackets, dashes and an ellipsis.

Typical mistakes

In the exam, students forget they can only be rewarded for the skills they show. You must include all the punctuation you can.

Students often fail to check their work – that is the stage when punctuation can often be improved.

Getting it right: Punctuating impressively

Examiners will be impressed if you can use punctuation with confidence and skill.

Mark scheme

Grades	Descriptors
7, 8, 9	A wide range of punctuation used accurately
5, 6	A range of punctuation, mostly successful
3, 4	A range of punctuation, with some control
1, 2	Some punctuation

There is extra credit for 'communicating imaginatively' – and punctuation can be used imaginatively too.

'Will you always remember me like this?' she cried. (Devastated, he remembered when she had once said, 'There will never be a time when I'll want to leave you ...'!)

Here, capitals, commas, a full stop, a question mark, an exclamation mark, brackets, speech marks and an ellipsis are all used accurately; and there are four elements of punctuation at the end, to impress.

Test yourself

Write three paragraphs telling the story of a sporting disaster. Include all the punctuation covered in this unit. Be imaginative if you can.

How to prepare for the exam

Make sure you include a wide range of punctuation in every piece of writing you produce.

Improving sentences and grammar

What this skill involves

Your sentences carry your message and you should vary them appropriately for what you want to say. You are marked on their effectiveness. So, you might use long sentences for description, short sentences to create drama, and so on.

What the examiner is looking for

The examiner is hoping to see:
- simple, compound and complex sentences
- sentences which are varied in construction
- sentences which communicate effectively.

In this unit you will revise:

- sentence forms
- how to use sentences to impress.

Getting it right: Sentence forms

REVISED

In any piece of writing, the examiner will be looking out for:
- simple sentences – contain one independent clause, which has a **subject** and a **verb**
- compound sentences – have two independent clauses, joined by a conjunction like 'and' or 'but'
- complex sentences – have independent clauses but also at least one dependent clause (which would not make sense on its own).

> **subject**: what the sentence is about or who performs the action
>
> **verb**: a doing word

This is an example from a descriptive response:

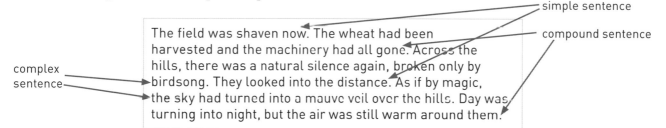

complex sentence → | simple sentence | compound sentence

The field was shaven now. The wheat had been harvested and the machinery had all gone. Across the hills, there was a natural silence again, broken only by birdsong. They looked into the distance. As if by magic, the sky had turned into a mauve veil over the hills. Day was turning into night, but the air was still warm around them.

Typical mistakes

Especially when writing descriptions and narratives, students often rely too heavily on compound sentences.

Without reading through a piece of writing carefully – as if reading it aloud in your head – it is hard to spot when sentences are not working well. Too few students check their work carefully; and few are willing to make the necessary improvements.

Exam tip

There is no need to worry about whether you are including all three forms as you write – but it is worth making sure they are all there when you check through at the end.

Task

1 Write a paragraph giving your views on the qualities – or otherwise – of television programmes. Use a mixture of sentence types. Consider:
   ○ beginning with a simple sentence which offers an opinion
   ○ following it with compound and complex sentences that explain your opinion.

Getting it right: Using sentences effectively

REVISED

It is not just a case of using different kinds of sentences – you need to use short and long sentences effectively. Notice how sentences have been used here:

> The girl's eyes caught Simon Templar as he entered the room, ducking his head instinctively to pass under the low lintel of the door; and they followed him steadily across to the bar. They were blue eyes with long lashes, and the face to which they belonged was pretty, crowned with yellow hair. She was the only girl in the place. She was still looking at him.
>
> Leslie Charteris, *Follow the Saint*, 1938

Two complex sentences set the scene, then two short simple sentences begin to suggest some drama to come.

Tasks

1 Imagine a scene when a stranger enters a room. Use longer sentences, then two or more short sentences to introduce tension.

In narrative writing particularly, you might want to use a **minor sentence** to add focus to a particular emotion or item. However, use such a technique sparingly.

minor sentence: sentence that is incomplete

minor ──────▶ Shock. Dismay. Everything she had lived for
sentences   had been taken from her in a moment …

You will also employ other techniques in Section B: rhetorical questions, exclamations, repetition for effect and so on. Aim always for variety, appropriateness and effect.

Consider this Grade 7 extract:

> Although we know that schools have better resources than in previous decades, they still need further investment. Incredibly, though, we have been told recently that there is no more money available; schools must cope with what they have. How can this be? In a world that requires more and more from school leavers, how can this underfunding be allowed? It is unacceptable.

2 Find:
   ○ rhetorical questions
   ○ a simple, compound and complex sentence
   ○ repeated phrasing.

Like this extract, you must use sentences effectively and accurately to get the best marks.

Mark scheme

Grade	Descriptors
7, 8, 9	● Uses a full range of sentences to create effects ● Has control of grammar
5, 6	● Uses a variety of sentences for effect ● Mostly controls the grammar
3, 4	● Attempts a variety of sentences ● Some grammatical control
1, 2	● Simple range of sentences ● Limited control of grammar

Test yourself

TESTED

Write the opening of a letter to your MP, telling them why your school needs extra funding.
Use a range of accurate and effective sentences.

How to prepare for the exam

- When reading, identify different kinds of sentences and decide how they have been used and why.
- In your own writing, aim for variety. Always check through and ensure the sentences work effectively.
- Practise writing extra paragraphs with ranges of sentences.

Vocabulary and crafting

What this skill involves

Part of your writing mark is for how well you use language: the quality of your vocabulary and how well you express yourself. You are expected to write in Standard English and, hopefully, demonstrate that you can use a wide range of vocabulary.

What the examiner is looking for

The examiner is hoping you will:
- write in correct standard English
- use an appropriate but ambitious vocabulary
- communicate imaginatively, crafting your language to make it interesting.

In this unit you will revise:

the effective use of:
- verbs and adjectives
- imagery
- rhetoric.

Exam tip

Always remember to aim to impress. Use the best words you know, rather than the ones that are easiest to spell. For example, spelling 'hole' correctly will gain you no marks for spelling; however, 'chasm' would get marks for vocabulary, even if it were spelt incorrectly.

Getting it right: Verbs and adjectives

REVISED

Notice the differences between these two extracts:

> He went down the long road. The night was cold and up ahead the hills were old and dark. He was afraid, but walked on.   (Grade 4)

> Bent and broken, he staggered down the seemingly endless road. The night was dismal and up ahead the hills frowned down at him, sullen and threatening. He shook with fear but stumbled forward.   (Grade 9)

Exam tip

Make sure you don't put an adjective before every noun: that makes your writing predictable and dull (e.g. 'The old man with the brown shoes had a pointed nose and carried a torn bag in his frail hand …').

Tasks

1 Write a new version, trying to match the Grade 9 standard but using different adjectives and verbs.
2 Write another three sentences with similarly imaginative vocabulary.

Getting it right: Imagery

REVISED

Imagery also enriches description and adds interest to narrative, and even to writing with a viewpoint. In particular, **similes** and **metaphors** can prove handy tools.

This is an extract from a modern American novel. A boy is on a long bus journey.

simile: a comparison, using 'like' or 'as'

metaphor: when something is not literally true

> The bus pulled out, like an animal waking from sleep … In Missouri, the countryside closed in, the road crowded by a mass of vegetation that filled the air with its rotting breath. The thick air would settle around me and I would struggle to breath, sometimes working myself into a panic, like a fish drowning on the deck of a boat.
>
> Brady Udall, *The Miracle Life of Edgar Mint*, 2001

Tasks

1 What does 'like an animal waking from sleep' make you imagine?
2 Think of two similes to describe a train quietly leaving a station.
3 The imagery builds in sentences 2 and 3. Find and explain the effects of:
   ○ the metaphors that help create the stifling atmosphere
   ○ the simile.
4 Write about walking into a room full of strangers. To explain how you felt, try to use:
   ○ two or three metaphors   ○ one or two similes.

Getting it right: Rhetoric

REVISED

Rhetoric is the art of using language to persuade. Notice how it works here:

emotive verb

repetition for effect

bright 'b's contrasted with depressing 'd' of dying

hopelessness with repetition of 'no' to end rhetorical question

> I have been dismayed by what I have seen in Syria. I have been dismayed by the weeping women, the starving children and the desperate fathers. Old people are shivering to death in this harsh winter; babies are being born to dying mothers. How long can the world stand back and offer no succour, no hope?

alliteration (woeful 'w's) and list of three powerful images

moving verb/image

Task

1 Write a paragraph in which you give your views on something about which you feel strongly. Use language that will make the reader agree with you. Use the best words you know and bear in mind the mark scheme for how you use vocabulary.

Mark scheme

Grades	Descriptors
7, 8, 9	Extensive and ambitious vocabulary
5, 6	Increasingly sophisticated vocabulary
3, 4	Varied vocabulary
1, 2	Simple vocabulary

Typical mistakes

● Overusing adjectives
● Forgetting to use imagery
● Offering a viewpoint without considering the effect of the language on the audience

Test yourself

TESTED

Write the opening of an article for a newspaper in which you give your views on the homeless in Britain. Make sure you use:
● rhetorical flourishes
● powerful adjectives and verbs
● imagery.

How to prepare for the exam

Take five minutes now and then and think of:
● adjectives and verbs you might use if describing ...
● similes you would use to describe ...

In each case, choose a person, place or event.

Paper 1, Writing to describe

What this question involves

On Section B of Paper 1, you will be offered the choice of two writing tasks. You must respond to just one of them. You might be given two descriptive tasks or two narrative tasks, or one descriptive task and one narrative task. Clearly, you need to be able to cope with both kinds of writing.

There are 40 marks for the question. 24 of those are given for the content of your response and how well you organise it; 16 marks are awarded for the quality of your sentences, punctuation and spelling, as well as on your ability to use the correct – and best – words.

You have 45 minutes to answer.

What the examiner is looking for

The examiner is hoping you will:
- produce interesting ideas that are well organised
- write accurately.

In this unit you will revise:

how to impress the examiner. You will focus on how to:
- describe people, places and events
- structure your descriptive writing
- use effective descriptive techniques.

Getting it right: Describing a person REVISED ☐

When describing people, you are likely to include their:
- physical appearance
- personality
- what they say and how they say it
- their actions and behaviour
- their thoughts: or others' thoughts about them.

Look at this description of a man. It is from a novel set in America.

> Behind him walked a huge man, shapeless of face, with large, pale eyes, with wide, sloping shoulders; and he walked heavily, dragging his feet a little, the way a bear drags his paws. His arms did not swing at his sides, but hung loosely and only moved because the heavy hands were pendula.
>
> He flung himself down and drank from the surface of the pool; drank with long gulps, snorting into the water like a horse. He dipped his whole head under, hat and all, and then he sat up on the bank and his hat dripped down on his blue coat and ran down his back. 'Tha's good,' he said. 'You drink some, George. You take a good big drink.' He smiled happily.
>
> John Steinbeck, *Of Mice and Men*, 1937

Notice that we immediately know about:

- his looks
- his clothing
- how he moves
- what he does
- his personality
- the way he speaks and what he says.

Tasks

1 From this extract, what do we suspect about the man?

2 He is like a 'bear' and 'like a horse': what is suggested by each of these details?

3 Choose someone you know. Write two paragraphs about them, suggesting as much about them as you can.

The writer allows us to make up our own mind about what the man is like.

It is often more subtle to 'show', rather than to just 'tell' and make judgments for the reader.

Task

1 Which of these is more interesting, and why?
  ○ She raised an eyebrow, smiled mysteriously, and took his hand.
  ○ She wanted to win him back so she took his hand.

Of course, it is possible to write interesting descriptions that tell the reader what a character is like – so long as the ideas are supported.

In this first-person narrative, a young boy describes his friend. Notice how we are presented with his opinions, but also how he justifies them by using examples of his friend's behaviour.

The two boys have been playing in the road with sticks and have tar on their clothes.

> Just as we were going in their gate, he said, 'If my mother wants to know how I got all this tar on, it was your stick that did it, not mine.' Just like him, blames it all on to me. Pinches my stick off me and then says it was my fault. He was my best friend was Ted, but I hated him sometimes. He was all right, but he was awkward in a lot of ways. It was always me that had to call round for him, never him that called for me. And he could hit you, but you couldn't hit him. And if he ever got into trouble, it was always your fault.
>
> Another thing about Ted, he was always saying things about people, but you just say anything about him and he used to turn on you. He used to come up to you and say: 'Do you want this button?' and if you said yes, well he used to pull it off your coat and give it to you, but if you said no, he used to pull it off and throw it away. Then he'd go: 'Well, you said you didn't want it!' You try anything like that with him, though. You never knew how far you could go with Ted.

Keith Waterhouse, *There is a Happy Land*, 1957

Annotations:
- personality/attitude: narrator's opinion
- stirs different feelings in narrator
- personality
- what he says
- personality
- his actions
- character is summarised by narrator

Whereas the first extract presented a character set in a scene, this is more to do with the writer's feelings and thoughts about his friend. Rather than describing how Ted looks and moves, it is a different approach: the narrator does not just show what they do – he also tells us what his friend is like.

Task

1 You have already described a person you know. Now produce one or two paragraphs explaining how you feel about them, supporting what you say with relevant details.

Exam tip

If you are describing a person, any approach is valid, but you must make sure you are producing a description and that you do not lose focus and begin to just write a story.

This description from a newspaper is less intimate:

> For the American music producer Pharrell Williams it was a huge moment. Last week he and Al Gore, Nobel peace prize winner and former US vice president, announced a concert over seven continents that is designed to build support for a UN climate pact in Paris at the end of this year.
>
> Pharrell, whose song 'Happy' was the bestselling single of 2014 and who was described by GQ magazine as 'a quiet little Egyptian space cat of a dude' is known for getting things done – at least in music …
>
> Ed Helmore, 'From spreading happiness to saving the planet, the rise and rise of Pharell', *The Observer*, 2015

Tasks

1 How is the first paragraph designed to catch our attention?
Think about:
○ the first sentence
○ the mention of Al Gore
○ what the two men are organising.
2 What does the second paragraph add?
3 What do you think we might be told next?

However the description is approached, it is crucial for it to be well structured and to involve interesting features, like the ones covered in the last few units. Ideally, you will have:
● an interesting opening
  ○ perhaps conversation, an anecdote or a vivid touch of description
● a development which looks at different aspects of the person or develops just one of their features
  ○ perhaps with sections on their looks and approaches to life, their history, their dreams or their despair …
  ○ and perhaps including imagery, quotations, examples of what they are like, others' opinions of them, sarcasm …
● an ending which brings everything neatly to a close, hopefully with a link back to the opening.

This is a Grade 9 opening to a description of Prince William.

At first glance, he seems like 'an ordinary enough guy'. He's got a broad smile, likes attending sporting occasions and has a beautiful wife. He seems to have it all: not least since the family fortune runs into hundreds of millions of pounds, he can stay in any number of castles, was given an £8 million helicopter by his grandmother and seems to have to do very little for the massive state benefits off which he lives. Of course, there are always two sides to any story.

introductory quotation/ assessment

positive list of three

list of luxuries enjoyed – apparently critical

introduces the rest of the response: could be positive or negative

Tasks

1 Write a final paragraph for the response, designed to interest the reader and link back to the opening.

2 Produce a detailed plan for this task:
Describe one of your parents or guardians.

Getting it right: Describing a place

There are three logical approaches to describing a place. You might:
- see the place as a photograph and describe what is there
- take a walk through the place and describe it as you go
- reflect upon the place and give your thoughts about it.

Or, you could:
- blend elements of each approach.

Once again, however, you should avoid turning your description into a story.

It will help if you:
- plan thoroughly
- begin and end effectively
- include engaging features – think especially about using:
  ○ the senses (sight, touch, taste, hearing and smell)
  ○ figurative language (especially similes and metaphors – but also consider alliteration and onomatopoeia)
  ○ rich vocabulary (including trying to include effective verbs, adjectives and adverbs)
  ○ snatches of conversation, perhaps.

Consider the contrast in effectiveness in these sentences:

Original	Improved
The room seemed strange.	The room smelt of fireworks and people could taste smoke in the air.
We were looking into a blue cave.	We were looking into a cave ablaze with rich colour, as blue as Krishna's skin.
The people went around the gardens calmly.	The people crept, hesitantly, around the gardens.

Tasks

1 Add detail based on the senses to the following:
  ○ As she walked in, she …
  ○ The weather had changed and now …

2 Add figurative language to each of the following:
  ○ Like … (simile), the church has stood there for centuries.
  ○ The fire … (metaphor), (metaphorical verb) … ing in the faces of the young children.
  ○ … . (alliteration) and … ing (onomatopoeia), the car made its way down the hill.

3 Add striking verbs, adjectives or adverbs to the following:
  ○ The old chair … (verb) beside the fire.
  ○ The students trooped … (adverb) into assembly.
  ○ A banner, … and … (adjectives), hung from an upstairs window.

4 Improve this Grade 3 extract. Try to bring it to life by including:
  ○ better verbs, and some adjectives and adverbs
  ○ at least one simile and one metaphor, and possibly onomatopoeia
    and alliteration
  ○ description based on the senses
  ○ extra detail where necessary.

> The park was quiet, even though the rain had stopped and it was sunny now. There was a woman with a small dog walking past the playground, but that was about all. The trees just moved in the breeze. The grass was green in the sunlight. Down by the pond, the ducks were quacking and moving their wings up and down.

It is a useful device, often, to move description from an overview, a general perspective, to a focus on something much more precise.

So, for example, you could describe a sporting event as if looking down on it from a great height, but then move in to describe the faces of the contestants.

This is part of a description of a seaside town from a Booker Prize-winning novel:

precise vocabulary →

> The town had been built in a shallow bay. The harbour lay on the south side. The trawlers would come in, unloading fish, seagulls drifting over in vast clouds above their decks, screeching, swooping to the water.

general view
detailed throughout
metaphorical verb and noun phrase

lively verb and onomatopoeia/ senses
second verb for effect – alliteration suggests they keep coming (with sudden, sweeping 's's)

move from general view of harbour to focus on the boy

metaphor →
rich vocabulary →
punctuation used to extend this sentence (just as his experience develops)

effective verb
sense of touch

> On the beach, a young boy gazed at the sea, half in fear, reluctant to go near it, watching it fold over in waves against the shore, the white spume, the suction of the water against the sand; and had finally gone down to it with his father, holding tightly to his hand, gasping as he felt his bare foot against the cold, stepping back, laughing, half-amazed, as he saw the children splashing through the waves.

precise verb choice

short phrases suggest his hesitation
touch of onomatopoeia?

list of verbs register his emotions
onomatopoeia

David Storey, *Saville*, 1976

This is from a student's Grade 8 description of Tromso, in the Arctic Circle.

> The snow was half a metre thick and still falling: sometimes dancing in the breeze, sometimes clumping down in huge flakes, as if it was all too heavy for the clouds to bear. Men worked tirelessly to clear paths around the town. Huge magical icicles hung from roofs, making the place like fairyland when you looked up, though below there were signs advising pedestrians to move off pavements into the road, in case any icicles fell: they were huge and they could spear you.
>
> Amazingly, the traffic still moved normally, though that was only possible because of the legal requirement to fit winter tyres. As ever in Norway, cars stopped obediently whenever and wherever anyone on foot wished to cross the road.
>
> My father shook his frozen hands ('My, oh my, it's chilly …') and hid behind the wheel of our rented Honda, wondering whether he dare set off. The mountain beside us, that we had to ascend, was steep and the shiny ice on the road seemed treacherous …

Tasks

1 What are the strengths of this description? Look out for:
   o metaphors and similes
   o impressive/appropriate verbs, adjectives and adverbs
   o sentence variety
   o the shift from general details to something more specific.

2 It is not necessary to write about faraway places: what might you do to this extract, describing a snowy day, to move it to a higher standard?
   Think about whether you could:
   o organise it better
   o add some of the same sorts of features you identified in Task 1
   o improve the vocabulary.

> When the snow came down, my mate and me headed straight to the park. It was full of other kids sledging and snowballing and throwing each other into the great white drifts. Excellent.
>
> In no time at all, my trousers were wet through and my gloves were soaked. Everyone was in the same state.
>
> Everywhere you looked there were tiny people running or falling into the deep snow. The hill was the best spot. If you went there, you could run down on your sledge all the way to the bandstand at the bottom.
>
> (Grade 4)

3 Write a better version of this description.

   With any description of a place, of course, structuring ideas is vital.
   You might decide to have:
   o an overview of the place
   o sections dealing with particular features of it
   o an ending that links back to the start but offers one final, new thought
   o people talking about the place
   o someone walking around it, describing as they go ...

Task

1 Plan and write a description of a shopping mall.

Getting it right: Describing an event

If asked to describe an event, you will be blending descriptions of people and a place. There might also be an element of narrative – if, for example, you describe a wedding, you will probably deal with the major incidents of the day – but you need to remember that you are writing a description, not a story.

Focus on the descriptive details.

This is a first-person description of a party at an American mansion in the 1920s.

movement, bustle → I wandered around rather ill at ease among swirls and eddies of people I didn't know. I was immediately struck by the number of young Englishmen dotted about; all well dressed, all looking a little hungry, and all talking in low voices to prosperous Americans.

outsider looking in, guessing → I was sure that they were selling something: bonds or insurance or cars.

judging what is happening → There was dancing now in the garden; old men pushing young girls backwards in eternal graceless circles, superior couples holding each other tortuously, fashionably, and keeping in the corners – and a great number of single girls dancing individualistically. By midnight the

atmosphere → hilarity had increased. A celebrated singer had sung in Italian and another had sung in

performances → jazz, and between the numbers people were doing 'stunts' all over the garden while happy,

continuing jollity – but 'vacuous', not genuine → vacuous bursts of laughter rose towards the summer sky.

F Scott Fitzgerald, *The Great Gatsby*, 1925

This extract captures a sense of the:
● people
● activities
● noise
● mood.

At the same time, the narrator is judging what is happening, interpreting it for the reader.

Tasks

1 Read this Grade 3 extract from a description of a party. Decide what you could add or improve to make it better.

It was good when we got there. Everybody was in the garden at first and they were cracking jokes and then they turned up the music in the living room. We went inside. There was no booze but there was coke. I had three cans. I was dancing with this bird called Janice and she was well fit. I liked it at first cos she kept laughing but Moz said she was laughing at me so I ditched her and went off with him for a smoke.

2 Write an improved version.

This is part of a third person Grade 9 description of a school Parents' Evening.

repetition for effect

Helping people to find different teachers in different classrooms in different blocks proved to be a different experience. The parents wandered round like lost souls, as usual, and student guides had quite an evening …

simile

leads into further description

It was hectic even before 6.30, when it was supposed to start. By 6.15, there was a man in hippy gear (Who wears a yellow flowered shirt and flares nowadays?) in reception, demanding 'to see the Principal right now' because 'he was not happy about the changes to school uniform, not happy at all!' He was taken aside and had his ego stroked by Mrs White, who must be the calmest Assistant Principal in the country. Then the mayoress arrived in a huge hat festooned with purple flowers and a floaty dress that seemed to take up most of the corridor when she moved. She was like a rudderless sailing ship. No one seemed sure why she was there, but she was given a cup of weak tea and a biscuit and settled down meekly in the principal's study.

When the main influx began, the guides lined up, took charge of any confused parents and led the poor confused dears along foreign corridors. Finally, they sat them on bought-new-for-the-occasion plastic chairs outside relevant rooms, in which the flustered teachers tried to explain why little Mohammed had only been graded C for homework or Steph had been given three detentions already this year, hardly glancing at the patient Mr and Mrs Patel or the fuming Mrs Moss as they tapped away at a laptop which they hoped would hold all the answers.

snatches of speech

simile

adverb: ambitious vocabulary

noun: ambitious vocabulary

patronising humour

effective adjectives

rhetorical question – with vivid detail

humorous metaphor

verb: ambitious vocabulary

humorous detail

metaphor

compelling detail

adjective: ambitious vocabulary

onomatopoeia: effective verb

The mark schemes should help you more fully understand what the examiner requires of you.

You are assessed on the content and organisation of your response and on your accuracy.

Content and organisation

Grades	Descriptors
7, 8, 9	• Writing is compelling with extensive and ambitious vocabulary • Perfectly matched to purpose, form and audience • Highly organised, and incorporating many complex ideas • Consistently well-organised paragraphs are linked fluently with integrated connectives
5, 6	• Clear and effective writing with increasingly sophisticated vocabulary • Clearly targeting purpose, form and audience • Interesting writing, with detailed and connected ideas • Suitable paragraphs throughout with connectives to link ideas
3, 4	• Mostly successful writing with varied vocabulary • Attempts to target purpose, form and audience • A variety of linked and relevant ideas • Some paragraphs and connectives
1, 2	• Simple communication of ideas with simple vocabulary • Simple awareness of purpose, form and audience • A few ideas, possibly linked • Random attempts at paragraphs, or no paragraphs at all

Assessment comment

This description maintains its entertaining, light-hearted approach throughout. The event is clearly visualised and the language used to describe it is 'compelling' (you want to read on …). Similes, metaphor, ambitious verbs and adjectives and other techniques are blended into a piece of writing which illustrates a strong Grade 9 performance.

Accuracy

Grades	Descriptors
7, 8, 9	● A wide range of punctuation used accurately ● Uses a full range of sentences to create effects and has control of grammar – Standard English consistent ● Extensive and ambitious vocabulary, spelt correctly
5, 6	● A range of punctuation, mostly successful ● Uses a variety of sentences for effect and mostly controls the grammar – mostly in Standard English ● Increasingly sophisticated vocabulary, generally spelt correctly
3, 4	● A range of punctuation, with some control ● Attempts a variety of sentences with some grammatical control – some Standard English ● Varied vocabulary with some accurate spelling of complex words
1, 2	● Some punctuation ● Simple range of sentences and limited control of grammar – occasionally in Standard English ● Simple vocabulary with accurate basic spelling

As with any other Section B response, planning is essential.

The description of the parent's evening was planned like this:

Opening (brief)

Parents struggling to find teachers – 'different' places – 'like lost souls': students are guides

Para 2

Early arrivals:

1. Angry hippy

Perhaps rhetorical question, humour, what he says (?)

2. Mad mayoress: flowery hat, floaty dress

Perhaps 'like a ship' (?), but looked after by Mrs Moss (turns meek)

Para 3

Main influx: patronise the parents (poor confused souls) – mention some and how they feel about their kids' performance – Mr and Mrs Patel, Mrs Moss

Mock the teachers? Glued to their laptops

Para 4

Principal 'stalking' the corridors and 'supporting the needy' (and avoiding the mayoress!)

Colon/semi-colons for what he tries to do (impress/help)

His speech in middle of evening ('ideas like dripping tap water and just as exciting': yawns all round)

Says hello to Mr and Mrs Sharma as he leaves the hall

Para 5

Mr and Mrs Sharma videoed for school website: their reflections on evening

Describe state of locker area, thoughts on labs etc. 'We don't want to criticise, but ...'

Lots of 'but's

Principal hovering throughout, clearly unhappy with what they say, but 'sporting a terrifyingly false grin'

Para 6

Everyone leaving (different doors, different cars, different reactions to what they've heard)

Steph Moss in for a difficult time when her mum gets home

Test Yourself answers at www.hoddereducation.co.uk/myrevisionnotes/gcse-english-language

In the same way that failure to plan affects any Section B response, the typical mistakes that students make also apply to all the tasks.

Typical mistakes

● Not planning, so the description is jumbled and ineffective
● Writing a story, rather than a description
● Writing too much, rather than displaying quality
● Not checking, correcting or improving the 'finished' article

Test yourself

TESTED

Plan and write a response to the following task:

Write a description of an assembly or a presentation event.

How to prepare for the exam

Practise planning: set your own tasks.

Practise writing short descriptions, full of the high-quality features you have been using in this unit.

Paper 1, Writing to narrate

What this question involves

On Section B of Paper 1, you will be offered the choice of two writing tasks. You must respond to just one of them. You might be given two descriptive tasks or two narrative tasks or one descriptive task and one narrative task. Clearly, you need to be able to cope with both kinds of writing.

If narrating, you are likely to have to write a short story, but might be set some other task – perhaps writing the opening section of a novel.

There are 40 marks for the question. 24 of those are given for the content of your response and how well you organise it; 16 marks are awarded for the quality of your sentences, punctuation and spelling, as well as on your ability to use the correct – and best – words.

You have 45 minutes to complete your answer.

What the examiner is looking for

The examiner is hoping you will:
- produce an engaging, well-organised story
- write accurately.

In this unit you will revise:

how to narrate. You will focus on how to:
- plan a narrative
- choose a **narrative perspective**
- include settings, characters and conversation
- begin and end your narrative impressively.

> **narrative perspective**: the point of view from which the story is told – e.g. omniscient, all-seeing narrator, or first-person narrator, or third-person narrator

Getting it right: Planning a narrative

REVISED

You will be given a title or a picture on which to base your story.

Because you have only a limited time available:
- do not try to write a whole novel – it's impossible
- limit yourself to just two or three main characters
- focus on just one or two scenes.

Bear in mind the most common way to structure a short story:
- establish a **situation**
- introduce a **trigger** which sparks the main events
- have some **conflict** connected to the trigger
- **build** the tension/excitement
- move to a **climax**
- often, add a **resolution** which offers an ending – probably just one paragraph.

> **Exam tip**
>
> Although just writing one or two scenes might seem limiting, it does allow you to present more detail – which makes it much more engaging for the examiner.

It can seem difficult to base a whole story around just a couple of scenes. However, it is possible to feed in other information about what has already happened using:

- conversation (e.g. 'I know we argued about this last week, but …')
- backfill (e.g. 'Although they had only been married two years …')
- other devices (e.g. 'The newspaper report had said it all …').

Consider how you might structure a story inspired by this picture:

Tasks

1 What are your characters like?
2 What might happen?
3 Where would the scene(s) take place?
4 What is the situation when your story begins?
5 What is the trigger for the problem?
6 How will you develop the conflict?
7 What will be the climax?
8 Will there need to be a brief resolution?
9 How will you divide it all into sections/paragraphs? Produce your plan.

Getting it right: Narrative perspective

REVISED

Sometimes, it works best to use:

- a first-person narrator – we tend to **empathise** more easily with them
- a third-person narrator – who can tell the story more **objectively**, possibly focusing on one character or being omniscient.

empathise: share the feelings of others

objectively: not influenced by personal emotions (opposite of subjectively)

This is a first-person narrative. In the story, a student has gone to visit his old teacher, who is sick.

> The minute I went in, I was sort of sorry I'd come. He was reading a boring magazine, and there were pills and medicine all over the place, and everything smelled like Vicks Nose Drops. It was pretty depressing. I'm not too crazy about sick people, anyway. What made it even more depressing, old Spencer had on this very sad, ratty old bathrobe that he was probably born in or something. I don't much like to see old guys in their pyjamas and bathrobes anyway. Their bumpy old chests are always showing. And their legs. Old guys' legs, at beaches and places, always look so white and unhairy.
>
> JD Salinger, *The Catcher in the Rye*, 1951

Tasks

1 What sort of a boy is speaking? What do we suspect about him?

2 Rewrite the story from an omniscient perspective.

3 Which version is best and why?

Now consider this third-person narrative.

A man who is mentally ill has told his wife he is tired and will go to bed early. She has been out.

> Lucy was late getting home to their hillside cottage; when she went upstairs, Eliot wasn't in their bedroom. Assuming that he was sleeping in the spare room, so that she wouldn't disturb him, she went to bed.
>
> An hour later, Lucy woke up with a premonition of disaster and went without getting dressed to the door of the guest bedroom; which, taking a deep breath, she opened. Half a second later, she slammed it shut again, and slumped heavily on the floor. He had been ill for more than two years, and all she could think of was *It's over.* When she started shivering she went back to bed and slept soundly until morning.
>
> He had sucked on his shotgun and pulled the trigger …
>
> Salman Rushdie, East, West, 1994

Tasks

1 What is suggested about their relationship?

2 What do we suspect about Lucy?

3 Explain what happened here from her viewpoint.

4 The two versions will be very different: which do you think is most effective, and why?

Your new version of the story will be very different if you have included her thoughts and feelings.

In the original version, her emotions are left for us to imagine; her behaviour is unexplained. In your first-person version, things are likely to be much clearer – though that is not what you always want when writing a narrative. You have to select the approach which works best for your purposes.

Of course, it is possible to write a third-person narrative in which the thoughts and background of a character – or characters – are perfectly clear.

Task

1 Write a paragraph from your story about the young people in the picture on p. 87 in three different ways:
   - using a first-person narrator
   - using a third-person narrator who does not directly reveal their feelings
   - using a third-person narrator who does include their emotions.

Getting in right: Settings, characters and conversation

REVISED ☐

In the unit on descriptive writing, you have already covered how to describe settings (pp. 79–81) and people (pp. 76–79). In narrative writing, you have to make things clear much more swiftly, or much more simply. Also, you are likely to blend the characters and settings, rather than dealing with them in totally separate paragraphs.

Here, a Grade 3 student tries to do exactly that.

> When he got to the market, he saw Kim who was in his class. She was pretty. He saw her in a crowd of people. They were all pushing to get to the stall where the cheap mp3 players were for sale. She said 'Hello, Jonty.'

A Grade 8 student reworked the extract:

> The market was a crush of bodies fighting their way between stalls which were selling everything from vegetables to electrical appliances and all at cut price. Finally, he caught a glimpse of Kim – her shining face, her excited eyes, coping somehow with the chaos all around her. She spotted him too as she was apparently being propelled towards the stall selling cheap and probably sub-standard mp3 players. She waved the usually friendly arm and shouted over the rabble in a voice that still had the accent of her native Thailand, 'Hello, Jonty!' before she disappeared again into the throng.

Tasks

1 In the second version – which is obviously much more detailed than the original – find:
   ○ what we learn about Kim ○ what we know about the setting.

2 Re-write this next Grade 4 standard extract, so that there is a clearer picture of the scene and what the characters are like.

> In the classroom, Majid and Khalid were talking. They were both sitting on desks, facing each other. Majid was bigger and said what they were going to do all the time. Khalid did as he was told.
>
> 'I hate this place' said Majid. He kicked the bin. 'It's a mess. Look at that rubbish piled over there.'
>
> Khalid looked at the heap of papers. It was next to the store-room door that badly needed painting. He still liked their form room really.

Although you need to take care not to write lengthy conversations, speech can be useful in short stories, because it adds to the other details to reveal what characters are like. As with writing to describe, it is often more effective to show, rather than tell.

Look at these extracts:

1 She was big and tough. Even the men on the estate treated her with caution. They avoided her when she was in one of her moods.

2 'Watch out. Liz is coming,' said Danny, stepping back into the shadows.

'Those muscles ...' said Al, moving to join him. 'She was in one of her tempers last week and she put that guy from Manor Road in hospital. She terrifies me sometimes. Pray that she doesn't see us.'

Task

1 Decide which extract is more interesting, and why.

Read this telephone conversation, taken from a novel.

'Can we meet? There're some things you said the other night that I wanted to go over.'

'I don't want ... I'm not ready to talk about it all again yet.'

'So what am I supposed to do in the meantime?' I know how I'm sounding – whiny, whingey, bitter – but I don't seem to be able to stop myself.

'Just ... live your life. You can't hang around waiting for me to tell you why I don't want to see you any more.'

'So, what happened to us maybe getting back together?'

'I don't know.'

Nick Hornby, *High Fidelity*, 1995

Tasks

1 What do we guess has happened?
2 Devise a plan for a short story in which this conversation has importance.

3 Imagine you are writing a narrative about rivalry between two families who live close to each other. Write a conversation of no more than 12 lines that shows what they think of each other and clarifies for the reader the sorts of problems they have had.

This is a Grade 9 standard response to the task.

'You,' said Zak, 'will leave here with broken legs.' He looked at Sam with blinding hatred.

'As if ...' Sam raised his voice and spoke to the whole pub. 'As if you could do anything to hurt me ...'

Sam hissed with venom. 'My dad died because of your family. My dad was beaten senseless because that mob from Stentham thought he was one of you. And you have the nerve to come in here ...'

'It wasn't my fault your dad was soft.' Zak laughed so everyone could hear him. 'But if you'd stayed out of our business, who would've cared? We run this manor. Don't you ever forget that.'

Tasks

1 What are the strengths of this response? Look at the:
  ○ variation in how the speech is presented
  ○ realism in how they speak
  ○ amount of background information that is being relayed
  ○ descriptive details that accompany the speeches.
2 Having read this response, could you improve yours? Re-draft it to improve the standard.

Getting it right: Openings and endings

As with all writing, the openings and endings of a narrative are vital.

The opening needs to interest the reader; the ending must leave a lasting impression.

Openings

Consider these openings:

1 On Wednesday afternoons the café served fish, Bangla style, and Clive always found it crowded with Bengalis. There was not only the usual young crowd who hung around the café day in and day out, but crews of older Bengali workers who came for the fish. Clive knew he could pick up leads for several stories from the café. Hoshiar Miah, the proprietor, whom the boys called 'Langda Miah', 'the lame one', would always drop him a hint of a story. Clive had become the *East London Herald*'s Asian specialist, and half his work was done in the Iqbal Café.

setting

main character

introduction to Clive's job

second character, introduced through characteristic

Clive's position

Farrukh Dhondy, *Come to Mecca*, 1978

Already, the reader suspects who the story will be about, where it might take place and something of the atmosphere.

2 What started it that night was the row Vince had with his father. He couldn't remember just what began the row itself, but something like it seemed to blow up every time the Old Man saw him, and started using expressions like 'idle layabout'. 'lazy good-for-nothing' and 'no-good young thug'. The Old Man never talked to you – he talked at you; he didn't carry on a conversation – he told you things. When Vince stormed out of the house he hardly knew where he was going he was so full of bottled up fury.

characters and conflict immediately

history of problem

touches of speech show father's attitude

the problem

sense of what is to come

how will it be released?

Stan Barstow, *The Human Element*, 1970

There is an immediate sense of the anger in Vince and what prompts it. The question to be resolved is where it might lead.

3 On the day of the miracle, Isabel was kneeling at the cliff's edge, tending the small, newly made driftwood cross. A single fat cloud snailed across the late-April sky, which stretched above the island in a mirror of the ocean below. Isabel sprinkled more water and patted down the soil around the rosemary bush she had just planted.

immediate hint of religion

suggests danger?

burial: who has died?

weather/mood

setting

'... and lead us not into temptation, but deliver us from evil,' she whispered.

prayer: is mention of 'temptation' and 'evil' significant?

M.L. Stedman, *The Light Between Oceans*, 2012

This is a more subtle opening, which sets the scene, gives an impression of Isabel and dangles possibilities of the story's likely themes.

In response to the title 'No room at the inn', this is how a Grade 3 student began.

> It was late and we couldn't find anywhere to stay. Dad said we will sleep in the car. Mum said she wouldnt. Then my sister said wed have to find a stable and we all laughed cept our Tim who said he didnt like animals and he would sleep in the car then.

Tasks

1 What other information would have been useful here?

2 What else could you have added to make it more interesting?

3 Make up a storyline of your own in response to the title.

4 Write three different openings. You should:
- ○ introduce one or two characters
- ○ include the setting
- ○ hint at what is to come.

You might begin with:
- ○ conflict
- ○ a conversation
- ○ an explanation of what someone is thinking and, perhaps, why
- ○ something dramatic.

Endings

It is difficult to appreciate how effective an ending is, unless you have read the whole story. However, note how these stories clearly come to a conclusion:

This is from a science fiction story about a man on his own in space, talking to the memory of his lover:

> You said to so many things, to so many loves, to so many dreams. ← romantic repetition
>
> sense of ending → 'Goodbye, Mary,' he said. 'Forgive me and God keep you.'
>
> He sat down at the table and pulled the journal that lay upon its top in front of him. He flipped it open, searching for the pages he must fill.
>
> his story will continue → He had work to do.
>
> conflicts resolved → Now he was ready for it.
>
> problem over → He had said his last goodbye.

Clifford Simak, *Way Station*, 1963

This ending is a mix of sadness and hope. Clearly, he has lost his love, but we realise that he can still move forward.

This ending is from a story about a television programme like *Big Brother*. The main character has become famous through it.

problem solved ———→ Coleridge felt a thrill of anticipation.
The lead part! He was to give the world his ←——— what is to come
Macbeth after all. Of course, Coleridge
wasn't stupid. He knew that he had only got ←——— something learnt
the part because he had been on television.
we are given his ——→ But why not? If everybody else could play the
thought game, why couldn't he? Fame, it seemed, *did*
message at ——→ have its uses.
the end

Ben Elton, *Dead Famous*, 2001

This ending is entirely positive, shows clearly that there has been resolution but also offers a message for consideration.

Here is a different kind of happy ending – to a horror story.

reaction to what———→ Childes shivered as he turned away, and breathed
has happened
presumably relief ——→ in deeply.
He slipped an arm around Amy's waist, ←——— romance/safety
relationship clear —→ pulling her gently to him, and they left that
terror left behind —→ haunted, silver lake.

James Herbert, *Moon*, 1985

This ending suggests relief but also togetherness. The evil is being left behind and a couple can leave together.

Of course, not all endings are happy. This unhappy ending came from a Grade 7 student:

> It was no good, I had lost him. I knew that straight away. Without even looking in my direction, he waltzed out of the door with Natalie and I knew I would never see him again. My heart sank and I had no idea how I was going to face the children. What could I tell them? How could I make it bearable?
>
> I should not have sent the note and I should not have begged him to come back. I am not a child any more, but I never learn.

Here, a Grade 6 student ends with a final paragraph that leaves the conclusion to the reader's imagination.

> The trek was now almost over, but she still had no idea whether she could survive. The training had not prepared her for situations like this. The rope bridge swung and as Codie clutched for a support to hold her safe, she heard snapping and knew that within moments she could be plunging into the canyon below. All she could do was rush on and hope.

Tasks

1 Think back to your story entitled 'No room at the inn'.
2 Write three endings:
   ○ a happy ending
   ○ a sad ending
   ○ an ending that leaves the reader to imagine what might happen next.

Exam tip

If you were asked in the exam to write the opening section from a novel, rather than a short story, you should approach the task in the same way: plan, include precise descriptions, conversations if appropriate and any other high-quality features.

The difference is that the ending will always leave some things 'in the air', to be developed later.

Typical mistakes

- Not planning, so the narrative is jumbled and unconvincing
- Inventing situations and settings that you have never experienced, so they are not credible
- Trying to include too many events, rather than concentrating on why and how things happen and on how things affect the character(s)

Test yourself

TESTED ☐

Write a story set in a modern city.

How to prepare for the exam

1 Practise planning stories that have a clear progression. Think:
   - situation,
   - trigger,
   - conflict,
   - build-up of tension/excitement,
   - climax,
   - resolution.

   Think of stories in terms of a ladder: you establish the grounding, then the tension builds as you climb. At the top, there will either be a happy or dramatically sad ending.

   Remember that you cannot maintain excitement throughout – you need to establish characters and settings, include dialogue if that is appropriate and build to the finish.

2 Practise writing effective openings and endings.

Climax

Building tension/ excitement

Situation

Test Yourself answers at **www.hoddereducation.co.uk/myrevisionnotes/gcse-english-language**

Paper 2, Writing with a viewpoint

What this question involves

On Section B of Paper 2, you will produce a response in which you give your views on a topic linked to the materials in Section A. Your audience and the form of your writing will also be made clear. So, for example, you might have to write a speech for parents, a letter to a Member of Parliament or an article for a broadsheet newspaper.

There are 40 marks for the question. 24 of those are given for the content of your response and how well you organise it; 16 marks are awarded for the quality of your sentences, punctuation and spelling, as well as on your ability to use the correct – and best – words.

You have 45 minutes to complete your answer.

What the examiner is looking for

The examiner is expecting you to:
- present a point of view clearly and persuasively
- write appropriately for the purpose and audience
- write accurately.

In this unit you will revise:

how to impress the examiner. You will focus on how to:
- write in the correct style and form
- produce a speech, article or letter
- write to persuade, using the most effective techniques in your response.

Getting it right: Writing in the correct style and form

REVISED ☐

You will be expected to write in Standard English: you must not respond to the task you are given in an informal, conversational style.

This is from a Grade 2 student, who is offering her views on whether it is acceptable to keep animals in captivity.

non-Standard English: 'really dangerous' →

> Animals should be free to go **were** they like but not if they are lyons or something because they would bite people. **Thats** **dead dangerus** so they should be kept in cages and not let out at all like bad criminals, only they arent they are just dum animals. But you cant have them all lose in towns **innit**? Perhaps they should be left in Africa so they don't hurt nobody.

spelling: 'where' problematic throughout
punctuation: 'that's'
informal

Tasks

1 In this response, some non–Standard English, technical errors and ideas have been picked out for you. Identify all the other:
   ○ elements of non–Standard English
   ○ spelling and punctuation errors.
2 Re-write the extract in Standard English and in a better organised form.

There is no certainty about exactly what you might be required to write in Section B of Paper 2, but speeches, articles and letters are likely forms.

Exam tip

If you have to write a blog entry, that could be problematic, because blogs take different forms and are often in **colloquial** English. However, remember that you are being assessed on the quality of your Standard English and make sure you are still writing formally.

colloquial: conversational, chatty

Getting it right: Speeches

REVISED

You might be told to write a speech. If so, you need to be aware of how to address your audience.

You might, for example:
- welcome them warmly ('Good evening, ladies and gentlemen …')
- challenge them ('As I look at you tonight, I cannot help but wonder if you have ever …')
- deliver a set of telling facts or figures ('In 1990, 87% of couples who lived together were actually married. Believe it or not, in 2015 …')
- use humour ('I used to have a full head of hair. Black hair. Then I began to support Leeds United. Now …')
- remind them of a relevant quotation ('None other than Martin Luther King once said …').

Exam tip

Always keep your audience in mind. We all speak to different people in different ways, and your ability to speak to them in the right way is being tested.

Tasks

Consider this task: **'Sixteen-year-olds should be allowed to vote: but first they need to be given some political education in schools.'**

1 Write a speech to be given to a youth parliament, in which you put forward your views on this proposal.

2 Copy out this table, then offer different openings for your speech, using the approaches listed.

Approach	Opening
anecdote	
statistics	
respectful	
using contrast	
humour	
sarcasm	

Ideally, your ending will summarise your views and win round the audience. You might say things like:
- 'Surely it is clear that …'
- 'I hope the case has been made; I cannot see how anyone could doubt that …'
- 'In years to come, when people look back on our attitude today …'

and/or possibly use:
- a significant quotation
- repetition for effect
- a list of three
- a rhetorical question or two.

3 Write your ending.

Test Yourself answers at **www.hoddereducation.co.uk/myrevisionnotes/gcse-english-language**

Getting it right: Articles

When writing an article, remember:

- there are no marks for illustrations – don't waste your time producing any
- it can be impressive to include suitable headings and sub-headings, but they are not essential: having interesting content in your text *is*
- if you do include headings, do not write in bubble-writing – that does not show a knowledge of the form
- resist dividing your page into columns: that almost always results in short sentences and paragraphs – and the mark scheme rewards you for using a range in both cases.

Read this extract from a newspaper article. Notice how the writer sets out to present his viewpoint in a way that interests the reader.

The naked rambler is making us look silly

Last week saw a flagrant attack on civil liberty mounted in the name of peace. A man who likes to walk around with a rucksack was told that he may have to spend the rest of his life in prison. ⟵ *contrast to begin*

surprising statement to generate interest

ambitious vocabulary

The rucksack, in this case, was not the cause of this draconian warning. It contained no bombs, real or fake. The problem was what the man, Stephen Gough, wore underneath the backpack: nothing. ⟵ *short, to shock*

Gough is better known as the Naked Rambler, an ex-marine who has spent most of the past seven years trekking around the countryside in nothing more than a pair of hiking boots and a hat. The rest of that time he has spent in police stations, courts and prisons. He has been arrested on more than 20 occasions, nearly every time in Scotland. ⟵ *begins to explain*

to make reader smile

What is it about Britain and nudity? Even in saunas we hold on to towels as though they were lifelines. Yet bare breasts are the wallpaper of tabloid culture, lap-dancing bars litter the nation's high streets and the most forensic pornography is available at the click of a mouse. ⟵ *challenges with rhetorical question*

simile ridicules the attitude

critical, emotive verb

⟵ *alliteration and metaphor put society's acceptance into context*

⟵ *cold, sounding unpleasant, unappealing*

Andrew Anthony, *The Observer*, 2010

The ending of an impressive article is always going to include the writer's main point.

Gough's behaviour is obviously unusual. ⟵ *summarising* But abnormal is not the same thing as criminal. While he has been adjudged to have broken the law, it's hard to see what crime he has committed. Any society that thinks prison is the correct place for him has lost grip of a basic principle of liberty. "Man is born free," wrote Rousseau, "but everywhere he is in chains." ⟵ *quotation used to draw viewpoint to a close*

opinion

ambitious vocabulary ——

In his own **eccentric** way, Stephen Gough has been trying to **break those chains**. He may be wrong, he may be misguided, but **he's not evil**. In treating him as though he were, the Scottish authorities have **got their knickers in a twist**. And that will prove far more damaging than not wearing any knickers at all.

what he thinks of the man ——

uses the same metaphor

colloquial phrase used for humour and because it's relevant to the subject

uses the phrase to hammer home the message and raise a smile

Andrew Anthony, *The Observer*, 2010

Task

1 Plan an article for a broadsheet newspaper to give your views on whether the royal family should be abolished.

In your plan, include some of the techniques from the Naked Rambler article, for example:
- ○ something surprising to catch the reader's attention at the beginning
- ○ a phrase to shock
- ○ humour
- ○ at least one simile and one metaphor
- ○ emotive language
- ○ quotation
- ○ impressive vocabulary
- ○ a memorable conclusion.

Getting it right: Letters

REVISED ☐

If you are asked to write a letter, it is almost certain to be a formal one – to a national figure, a newspaper, the BBC or some other organisation.

You need to know how to set it out properly. This is the traditional way:

9 Dovecot Avenue
Kibworth
Leicestershire
LC17 0JH
← Top right: your address

9 June 2015
← Beneath: the date

Address on left: the person you are writing to and their address ——→

Ms Hazel Bland
House of Commons
London
SW1A 0AA

Dear Ms Bland: customary opening ——→

Dear Ms Bland,

To finish:

Dear Ms Bland, (or any time you use a name) ends:

Yours sincerely,

Dear Sir, (or Madam,) ends:

Yours faithfully,

Exam tip

It's easy to know whether to use 'faithfully' or 'sincerely': remember that when you hold two bar magnets, the south poles never go together. Here, you also have two 's's – 'Dear Sir' and 'Yours sincerely'. They don't go together either.

If you are writing a letter, you can use the same range of techniques that you might use in speeches or articles.

However, you will be addressing one person directly, so you might well decide to avoid:
- grand rhetoric (as if you were trying to stir a huge crowd e.g. 'We need to stand tall! We need to go from this place and prepare for government …')
- any appeal to a mass audience (e.g. 'We all need to think about how we spend our days and whether the children of this country are suffering …').

Instead, you can personalise the ideas, while still keeping the formality:
- 'I hope you will realise it is time for you to step forward and start to prepare for government.'
- 'You might even ask yourself whether you are spending days usefully and whether your own children are suffering.'

> **Exam tip**
>
> You **might** use the second-person technique in speeches or articles; you will **always** use it in a letter.

Tasks

1 Compare the opening paragraphs in these two letters. They are written to the Prime Minister to offer views on whether we should change the way our country is governed. Decide why:
- Letter 1 appears to be from a Grade 2 student
- Letter 2 is reaching Grade 9 standard.

To help, look back at the mark scheme on page 83.

Letter 1

Dear Mr Prime minister, this country is a mess and you know that and its about time you did something about it and got it sorted right. My mum sas shes not got enug money and nether have I so we need lots more and we shuld be able to say what needsd doing. Think on

---

Letter 2

Dear Sir,

Since coming into office, you have prioritised the need to modernise this country. The United Kingdom cannot afford to stand still, because to do so would be to allow the rest of the world to leave us behind – in terms of trade, and economic and social progress and in the furtherance of human rights. We have to be moving through the twenty-first century with confidence and with pride in our achievements. You know these things.

However, I am hoping that you will take the next step in the full democratisation of the UK and begin to allow ballots on those important changes that affect us all. Referenda must, surely, become part of our everyday life, so that the public can feel involved and can begin to feel that they are part of decision-making.

In Letter 2, you should have noticed:
- the formal second-person approach
- subtle flattery
- the ambitious vocabulary
- a list of three
- the variety in sentences
- the strong persuasive approach (including 'surely')
- the logical and effective development of ideas.

2 Plan and write a letter of your own to the Prime Minister about the need to make our country a fairer place for everyone.

> **Exam tip**
>
> In the exam, you can use ideas from Section A in your response, but avoid copying. Do not 'lift' parts of the text – apart from facts and figures, obviously. Use your own words whenever you can.

Getting it right: Writing persuasively

It is obvious that when anyone presents a point of view, they hope the audience will accept it. To be successful, you should be drawing together the skills you have revised in this unit and throughout the other units on Section B responses.

Your chances of persuading the audience will hinge on a number of factors:

- how well you engage the audience
- 'seeing' the audience and making sure you address them appropriately
- using Standard English
- the quality of the ideas
- presenting, perhaps, four or five significant ideas, each well explained
- using a structure that has been planned and so is logical, demonstrating 'joined-up thinking'
- the overall quality of the writing
- your accuracy
- using a wide range of vocabulary, paragraphing and sentences
- how interesting you make the ideas
- the high-quality features you include such as statistics, quotations, examples and anecdotes, lists, similes and metaphors, rhetoric, humour …

Task

1 Consider this extract from a response offering views on the way old people sometimes behave and how it might be made more interesting. Then, complete the table, making additions to enrich the ideas.

> Some old people are just incredibly bad mannered ..A.. In fact, they can behave so much worse than the teenagers they spend so much time criticising ..B.. It is so frustrating for anyone under the age of twenty that they have to suffer the abuse without responding because they are not considered old enough to have an opinion on anything ..C..

	Possible additions
	You might add a simile, statistics, a quotation, sarcasm … Offer as many alternatives as you can in each case.
A	
B	
C	

Test Yourself answers at **www.hoddereducation.co.uk/myrevisionnotes/gcse-english-language**

This is part of a television review, in which the writer gives his views on *Doctor Who*.

exaggerated metaphor →

After months of being whipped into a frenzy of anticipation by the BBC's marketing department, I was disappointed to find myself slipping out of consciousness during the thrill-free early scenes of the new *Doctor Who*. Admittedly, we had the momentary distraction of a massive roaring dinosaur wading threateningly down the Thames (my heart went out to the hardworking CGI team when the poor creature had to be burned to death after five minutes on the grounds of plot irrelevance), but Peter Capaldi as the latest Time Lord must have been wondering what he'd got himself into as he capered around Victorian London in a nightgown, spouting nonsense for a good half hour. Had he regenerated himself as a person with dementia? It was hard to say. Certainly he didn't appear to be himself, but he wasn't Matt Smith either – and where did that leave his young assistant, Clara, so rudely deprived of a flirt-buddy nearer to her own age?

← exaggeration for effect

metaphor →

vivid verb → capered

opinions →

sarcasm → dementia

poking fun → flirt-buddy

Phil Hogan, *The Guardian*, 2014

This review offers views on *Doctor Who*. It relies heavily upon:
● exaggeration
● metaphor
● humour.

It is intended to convince the readers by making them smile. This approach is totally suitable in a newspaper's television review.

> **Exam tip**
>
> If you are asked to write a review, treat it as a kind of article, but often the intention is to entertain the readers.

Task

1 Write a review of your favourite television programme or computer game. You do not have to use humour, but try to structure your review so that you include things like:
  ○ characters
  ○ settings
  ○ storyline
  ○ outstanding or disappointing features
  ○ why you would or would not recommend it.

The review of *Doctor Who* is light-hearted. When people feel that something is more important, they are much more serious.

> The dreadful murders of PCs Nicola Hughes and Fiona Bone in Manchester have, understandably, caused some people to question whether Police in the UK should be routinely armed. I do not think they should be armed.
>
> I am not a Police Officer any more and no longer face the challenges and the dangers of the job and serving Officers are entitled to their own view on this issue since they still have to go to calls not really knowing what hazards they may face.

But it seems that even serving Officers are usually against being armed – a survey in 1995 of serving officers found that 79 per cent were against the routine arming of Police and I suspect that even now the majority of them would not want to carry a gun.

Arming all Police Officers would bring many problems. There are around 100,000 Officers in the UK – obviously not all would carry guns but let's say we had 10,000 Officers routinely carrying a gun – that's an extra 10,000 firearms on UK streets with all the dangers that would bring.

As good as any training might be, Officers would make mistakes – people would be shot – accidents would happen …

Bob Morgan, *The Huffington Post*, 2012

Notice here the use of:
- two contrasting points of view
- how one point of view is stressed and supported
- the use of statistics
- the use of facts and figures to support the writer's viewpoint
- the movement to a very convincing final point.

Test yourself

TESTED ☐

Decide whether you think it would be wise to arm the police.

Create a spider diagram of ideas.

Transform that spider diagram into an organised list. Remember to include jotted reminders to show how you will make your opinions more convincing: similes, quotations, examples …

In just thirty minutes, as an exam practice, write your response.

Check your 'finished' version carefully, and correct and improve it as necessary.

Typical mistakes

- Jumbling ideas because the response has not been carefully planned and checked
- Offering ideas that are unconvincing because they are just stated, without any evidence or interesting features to support them
- Losing focus on the title

How to prepare for the exam

Read articles in newspapers and magazines that offer a point of view. It is valuable, for example, to read sports articles, television reviews or problem pages: anywhere where the writer is offering viewpoints.

Underline the features of the articles which are making them convincing.

Practise planning and writing responses of your own: choose your own subjects because any practice is valuable since you are using the same skills whether you are giving your views on world affairs or whether *Coronation Street* is really the best show on terrestrial television.

How to do extra revision for the exam

I don't need to practise for English, do I?

Obviously, if you have worked through this book, you will be well prepared for the exam itself. However, it is sensible to build on the practices you have already completed: and you can revise thoroughly for English Language very easily – and almost always in neat, five-minute sessions! What could be more manageable?

The key is to focus on each question in turn and remind yourself of exactly what the examiner is looking for. That is not as difficult as it seems, because the exam papers are so predictable.

Organise a timetable so that:

- if you are six months away from the exam, you spend five minutes each day on your English, working on a different skill each time
- if it is three months from your Big Day, spend 2 × 5 minutes each day
- if you are just a month away from the exam when you start revising, ideally you will be spending 6 × 5 minutes each day.

So, exactly how do I practise?

There is advice in each unit in the book, but each of these activities is 'do-able' in 5 minutes:

Paper 1, Section A

Q1	Finding details	Read the opening page of a novel or the first paragraphs of a magazine story. Find details that tell you about a character or the setting or what is happening.
Q2	Writing about language	Choose two paragraphs from a story and ask yourself: If I were in the exam, which bits of language would I write about? What would I say about them? Jot down notes, if you want to – but the exercise can be done in your head.
Q3	Dealing with structure	Take a section of a story and decide how it has been put together: What makes the opening interesting? How does it develop? Do we get an increasing knowledge of a character? Are there contrasts? Or surprises? Do the words link to create an ongoing impression? Are the sentences used for effect? Are the paragraphs used for effect?
Q4	Evaluating writers' methods	Choose an opening and ask yourself: How good is it? Why? Look at how the writer has tried to interest you (with words, actions, techniques). At another time, ask yourself whether you are supposed to like a particular character, or despise her and why and how that impression has been created. Next time, what is the theme or themes and how successfully are they put across? Or, how is the setting made clear and interesting?

Paper 2, Section A

Q1	Finding what is true	Work with a friend. Ask them to find 4 things in a newspaper article which are true (some might be things that are being suggested); ask them to write them down – and to also write 4 things which are close to being true, but aren't really. You then decide which 4 things are true and not just opinions or simply incorrect.
Q2	Dealing with two texts and summarising	It is hard to find two texts that can be compared: but you can always practise summarising the main points in just one text. In this case, just jot down some quick notes. If you can find two reports of the same thing – perhaps of a demonstration or a tragic accident – you can draw up a quick grid, and put the comparable features next to each other.
Q3	Analysing the effect of language	As with Paper 1, Q2, find a short text and decide what you would write about and what you should say. In this case, you will be using a non-fiction text: one from a newspaper will be fine.
Q4	Comparing two sources and writers' methods	As with Q2, you can practise the basic skill on just one source. Ask yourself: what methods is the writer using to put across a message? If you have two articles or reports on the same subject, you can again draw up a quick practice grid and put points of comparison next to each other.

Section B (both papers)

	Organising your writing	Make up a title and spend 5 minutes producing a detailed plan for it. On another occasion, write an attention-grabbing opening for it. On another occasion, write an impressive ending that links with the opening.
	Effective punctuation	Write a couple of paragraphs – perhaps from a description – and try to get in all the punctuation you know.
	Improving sentences	Take one of the paragraphs you have written and rewrite it, with more sentence variety, as appropriate.
	Using impressive vocabulary	Each week, consider learning five new words and their meanings – words that are impressive and which you might not normally use, e.g. stigmatise, chasm, idyllic … You then hope you might have the opportunity to use some of them in your exam responses.
P1, Q5/6	Writing to describe	Plan a description. Next time, write a paragraph from it, making the standard as high as you can manage. Write an opening; then, at another time, an ending.
P1 Q5/6	Writing to narrate	Plan a story. As with description, write an opening (introducing a character/setting/situation …) and, later, an ending … and at another time write a revealing extract of conversation.
P2, Q5	Writing with a viewpoint	Decide on an issue that interests you, then repeat the plan/opening/ending practices.

All of this is not nearly as hard as it looks. But the sooner you start, the better!

You can also complete the practice activities in the Hodder Education Workbook by author Keith Brindle, which will give you an enormous boost.

AQA English Language Workbook: 9781471833946.